GREEK AND ROMAN ATHLETICS
A Bibliography

GREEK AND ROMAN ATHLETICS
A Bibliography

With Introduction,
Commentary and Index

BY

THOMAS F. SCANLON
University of California, Riverside

ARES PUBLISHERS, INC.
CHICAGO MCMLXXXIV

First Edition

ARES PUBLISHERS, INC.
7020 NORTH WESTERN AVENUE
CHICAGO, ILLINOIS 60645

ISBN 0- 89005-522-X

PREFACE

An extensive bibliography covering both Greek and Roman athletics and including works from as early as 1573 (Mercurialis, 107 below) to the present cannot be absolutely complete. This is due somewhat to the interdisciplinary nature of the topic, to the occasionally obscure and scattered sources, and to deliberate selectivity. But such a comprehensive research tool long overdue for students and scholars in a growing field should foster research and teaching at all levels. Readers are invited to send the author bibliographical references for inclusion in a possible later edition.

The speed with which this work was completed is due to the wonders of modern technology. The text of the bibliography was entered onto 8-inch discs via Xerox 820 computer and word-processor. The introduction and author index are on 5.5-inch discs of a Lexitron VT 1202.

I wish to thank the Academic Senate of the University of California at Riverside for their generous support of my research on ancient athletics through research grants. My great personal thanks are due to my research assistant, Andrew Schacht for typing entries on the word processor, tracking down numerous references, and entering countless corrections on the manuscript. His care and diligence added much to the quality of the work. My thanks also to Professor George Eisen who added the translations of Hungarian titles. I am most grateful to Eileen Conrad and Linda Lambert for entering and revising the introduction and author index on the Lexitron. Many thanks are also due to Al Oikonomides and the staff of his Ares Press for their care, diligence and encouragement. Finally I give very special thanks to Wendy, my colleague and wife, for her proof-readings, her many useful suggestions, and most of all, her patience with and encouragement in this project. It is to her that this work is dedicated.

University of California, Riverside — Thomas F. Scanlon

CONTENTS

ABBREVIATIONS

AA	Archaeologischer Anzeiger. Berlin.
AAA	*Ἀρχαιολογικὰ Ἀνάλεκτα ἐξ Ἀθηνῶν.* Athens.
AAHG	Anzeiger fuer Altertumswissenschaft, ed. by Oesterreichischen Humanistischen Gesellschaft. Innsbruck.
AAntHung	Acta Antiqua Academiae Scientiarum Hungaricae. Budapest.
AAWW	Anzeiger der Oesterreichischen Akademie der Wissenschaft in Wien, Philos.-Hist. Klasse. Vienna.
ABSA	Annual of the British School at Athens. London.
AC	L'Antiquité Classique. Louvain.
ACR	American Classical Review. City University of N. Y.
AD	*Ἀρχαιολογικὸν Δελτίον.* Athens.
AE	*Ἀρχαιολογικὴ Ἐφημερίς.* Athens.
AEA	Archivo Español de Arqueología. Madrid.
AEAA	Archivo Español de arte y arqueología. Madrid.
AEHE 4e Sect	Annuaire de l'École pratique des Hautes Études, IVe section, Sc. hist. et philol. Paris.
AHR	American Historical Review. New York.
AIHS	Archives Internationales d'Histoire des Sciences. Paris.
AJA	American Journal of Archaeology. New York.
AJAH	American Journal of Ancient History. Cambridge, Mass.
AJPh	American Journal of Philology. Baltimore.
AKG	Archiv fuer Kulturgeschichte. Cologne.
AncSoc	Ancient Society. Louvain.
Ant	Die Antike. Berlin.
AncW	Ancient World. Chicago.
AnzAW	Anzeiger fuer Altertumswissenschaft. Innsbruck.
AP	L'Année Philologique. Paris.
APF	Archiv fuer Papyrusforschung und verwandte Gebiete. Leipzig.
ArchClass	Archeologia Classica. Rivista dell'Istituto di Archeologia dell'Università di Roma. Rome.
Arch.(Sofia)	Archéologie. Sofia, Académie des Sciences, Inst. et Musées archéologiques.
ARID	Analecta Romana Instituti Danici. Copenhagen.
ASAA	Annuario della Scuola Archeologica di Atene e delle Missioni Italiane in Oriente. Rome.
AT	Antik Tanulmányok - Studia Antiqua. Budapest.
A&A	Antike und Abendland. Berlin.
AW	Antike Welt. Zurich.
BAGB	Bulletin de l'Association G. Budé. Paris.
BBF	Bulletin des Bibliothèques de France. Paris.
BCH	Bulletin de Correspondance Hellénique. Paris.
BCO	Bulletin Classica Orientalis. Berlin.
BCTH	Bulletin Archéologique du Comité des Travaux Historiques. Paris.

BELL Bulletin de la Société des Études des Lettres. Lausanne.
BHM Bulletin of the History of Medicine. Baltimore.
BIAB Bulletin de l'Institute Archéologique Bulgare. Sofia.
BICS Bulletin of the Institute of Classical Studies of the University of London. London.
BJ Bonner Jahrbuecher des Reinischen Landesmuseums in Bonn und des Vereins von Altertumsfreunden in Rheinlande. Bonn.
BMCR Bulletino del Museo della Civilta romana. Rome.
BO Bibliotheca Orientalis. Leiden.
BRL Bulletin of the John Ryland's Library. Manchester, England.
Bull.Offic.du Comité Internat. Olymp. Bulletin Officiel du Comité International Olympique.
ByzZ Byzantinische Zeitschrift. Munich.
CAF Citius Altius Fortius. Estudios Deportivos. Madrid.
CB The Classical Bulletin. Saint Louis, MO.
CE Chronique d'Égypte. Brussels.
CEA Cahiers des Études anciennes. Montreal.
CJ The Classical Journal. Boulder, Colorado.
CPh Classical Philology. Chicago.
CQ Classical Quarterly. Oxford, England.
CR Classical Review. Oxford, England.
CRAI Comptes rendus de l'Académie des Inscriptions et Belles Lettres. Paris.
CSCA California Studies in Classical Antiquity. Berkeley.
CW The Classical World. Pittsburgh, PA
DA Dissertation Abstracts. Ann Arbor, MI
Doss Arch Dossiers de Archéologie. Documents. Archeologia. Paris.
DLZ Deutsche Literaturzeitung fuer Kritik der Internationalen Wissenschaft. Berlin.
D.-S. Dictionaire des antiquités grecques et romaines. Ed. par Ch. Daremberg, E. Saglio, E. Pottier, and I. Lafaye. Paris, 1877-1929.
Dt.mediz. Wochenschr. Deutsche medizinische Wochenschrift.
DT-Z Deutsche Turn-Zeitung. Blaetter fuer die Angelegenheiten des gestammten Turnwesens. Leipzig.
EAZ Ethnographisch-archaeologische Zeitschrift. Berlin.
EClás Études Classique. Aix-en-Provence.
EEThes Epistemonikē Epeterìs tē̃s philosophikē̃s Skolē̃s toũ Aristoteleĩou Panepistemĩou Thessaloníkes. Thessalóniki.
EMC Échos du Monde classique. Classical News and Views. Otawa.
Enc. It. Enciclopedia Italiana.
Festgabe Mehl Zur Weltgeschichte der Leibesuebungen. Festgabe fuer Erwin Mehl zum 70. Geburtstag. R. Jahn, ed. Frankfurt, 1960.

F&F Forschung und Fortschritte. Berlin.
G&R Greece and Rome. Oxford, England.
GArb Geistige Arbeit. Zeitung aus der wissenschaftlichen Welt. Berlin.
GB Grazer Beitraege. Zeitschrift fuer die klassische Altertumswissenschaft. Graz.
GBA Gazette des Beaux-Arts. Paris.
GIF Giornale Italiano di Filologia. Rivista trimestrale di Cultura. Naples.
GRBS Greek, Roman, and Byzantine Studies. Durham, N. C.
HAnt Hispania antiqua. Rivista de historia antiqua. Valladolid, Spain.
HED The History, Evolution, and Diffusion of Sports and Games in Different Cultures. Proceedings of the Fourth International HISPA Seminar. R. Renson, P. P. de Nayer, and M. Ostyn, eds. Brussels: 1976.
HfL Hochschullblatt fuer Leibesuebungen. Zeitschrift fuer die Fragen der Koerpererziehung an Hochschulen und Hoehern Schulen.
HG Humanistisches Gymnasium. Leipzig.
HJ Historisches Jahrbuch. Munich.
HSCP Harvard Studies in Classical Philology. Cambridge, Mass.
HT History To-day. A monthly magazine. London.
HZ Historische Zeitschrift. Munich.
ICS Illinois Classical Studies. Urbana, Champaign, and Chicago, IL.
IJNA International Journal of Nautical Archaeology and Underwater Exploration. London.
Jahrb.d.I. Jahrbuch des Deutschen Archaeologischen Instituts. Berlin.
JCPh Jahrbuecher fuer classische Philologie.
JHS Journal of Hellenic Studies. London.
JOeAI Jahreshefte des Oesterreichischen Archaeologischen Instituts. Vienna.
JRS Journal of Roman Studies. London.
JSH Journal of Sport History. NASSH Univ. Park, Pennsylvania.
JThS Journal of Theological Studies. Oxford, England.
KBSW Koelner Beitrage zur Sportwissenschaft. Schorndorf, W. Germany; from vol. 6, St. Augustin.
KP Der Kleine Pauly. Lexicon der Antike auf der Grundlage von Paulys Realencylopaedie der klassischen Altertumswissenschaft. Five vols. Stuttgart: 1964-1975.
LEC Les Études Classiques. Namur, France.
LF Listy Filologické. Prague.
LKE Leibesuebungen und koerperliche Erziehung. Berlin.
LZB Literarisches Zentral-Blatt. Leipzig.
MC Il Mondo Classico. Torino.
MDAI(A) Mitteilungen des Deutschen Archaeologischen Instituts (Athen. Abt.). Berlin.

MDAI(R)	Mitteilungen des Deutschen Archaeologischen Instituts (Roem. Abt.). Mainz.
MEFR	Mélanges d'Archéologie et d'Histoire de L'École Française de Rome. Paris.
MH	Museum Helveticum. Revue Suisse pour l'Étude de l'Antiquité classique. Basel.
Mod.Lang. Journ.	Modern Language Journal. National Federation of Modern Language Teachers. Boulder, Colo.
MPh	Museum. Maanblad voor Philologie en Geschiednis. Leiden.
N&C	Nigeria and the Classics. Ibadan.
NASSH Proceedings	North American Society for Sport History Proceedings.
NAWG	Nachrichten der Akademie der Wissenschaften in Goettingen, Philol.-Hist. Klase. Goettingen.
NRS	Nuova Rivista Storica. Rome, Soc. Ed. Dante Alighieri.
NSA	Notizie degli Scavi di Antichità. Rome.
NTSuppl.	Novum Testamentum. An International Quarterly for New Testament and Related Studies. Supplement. Leiden.
NYRB	New York Review of Books. Milford, Conn.
Oesterr. Jahresh.	Oesterreichische Jahreshefte. Vienna.
Olympische Rdsch.	Olympische Rundschau.
OMS	L. Robert, *Opera Minora Selecta*. Four vols. 1969-1974.
PAA	*Πρακτικὰ τῆς Ἀκαδημίας Ἀθηνῶν*. Athens.
PAAH	*Πρακτικὰ τῆς ἐν Ἀθήναις Ἀρχαιολογικῆς Ἑταιρείας*. Athens.
PCA	Proceedings of the Classical Association. London.
PCPhS	Proceedings of the Cambridge Philological Society. Cambridge, England.
PhW	Philologische Wochenschrift. Leipzig.
Prométhée, Rev. d'Éd.	Prométhée, Revue d'Éducation ed. par les Amis de l'École Norm. Ch. Buls. Brussels.
QAL	Quaderni di Archeologia della Libia. Rome.
QUCC	Quaderni Urbinati di Cultura classica. Rome.
RA	Revue Archéologique. Paris.
RACF	Revue archéologique du Centre (de la France). Vichy.
RAL	Rendiconti della Classe di Scienzi morali, storiche, e filologiche dell'Accademia dei Lincei. Rome.
RB	Revue Bénédictine. Abbaye de Maredsous, Belgium.
RBPh	Revue Belge de Philologie et d'Histoire. Mechelen.
RCCM	Rivista di Cultura classica e medioevale. Rome.
RE	Paulys Real-Encyclopaedie der klassischen Altertumswissenschaft. Neue Bearbeitung von G. Wissowa. Stuttgart, 1894-1970. Munich, 1970-present.
REA	Revue des Études Anciennes. Talence.
RecSR	Recherches de Science Religieuse. Paris.
REG	Revue des Études Grecques. Paris.

REL Revue des Études Latines. Paris.
RFIC Rivista di Filologia e di Istruzione Classica. Torino.
RhM Rheinisches Museum. Frankfurt.
RHS Revue d'Histoire des Sciences et de leurs applications. Paris.
RIA Rivista del'Instituto Nazionale de Archeologia e Storia del'Arte. Rome.
RIL Rendiconti del'Instituto Lombardo, Classe di Lettere, Scienze morali e storiche. Milan.
RLAC Reallexicon fuer Antike und Christentum. Stuttgart.
RPAA Rendiconti della Pontificia Accademia di Archeologia. Rome.
RPh Revue de Philologie. Paris.
RPhilos Revue Philosophique. Paris.
RS Revue de Synthèse. Paris.
RSC Rivista di Studi Classici. Torino.
San Journal of the Society of Ancient Numismatics. Santa Monica, California.
SAWW Sitzungsberichte der Oesterreichischen Akademie der Wissenschaft in Wien, Philos.-Hist. Klasse. Vienna.
SDHI Studia et Documenta Historiae et Iuris. Rome.
SE Studi Etruschi. Florence.
StudClas Studii Clasice. Bucharest.
StudSal Studii Salentini. Lecce.
TAPA Transactions and Proceedings of the American Philological Association. Cleveland, Ohio.
TCWA Transactions of the Cumberland and Westmoreland Antiquarian and Archeological Society. Kendal, England.
TLS The Times Literary Supplement. London.
VDI Vestnik Drevnej Istorii. Revue d'Histoire ancienne. Moscow.
Vet Chr Vetera Christianorum. Bari, Italy.
WB Weiner Blaetter fuer die Freunde der Antike. Vienna.
WPr. Berlin Wincklemannsprogramm der archeologischen Gesellschaft zu Berlin. Berlin.
WS Weiner Studien. Zeitschrift fuer klassische Philologie und Patristik. Vienna.
WZ Halle Wissenschaftliche Zeitschrift der Martin-Luther-Univ. Halle-Wittenberg.
WZ Rostock Wissenschaftliche Zeitschrift der Univ. Rostock, Gesellsch.-und sprachwiss. Reihe. Rostock.
ZAnt Ziva Antika. Antiquité vivante. Skopje, Yugoslavia.
ZPE Zeitschrift fuer Papyrologie und Epigraphik. Bonn.

INTRODUCTION

This work was occasioned by my own initial difficulty in finding adequate bibliographical resources for teaching and research in the field of Greek and Roman athletics. As a classicist I found that even the standard bibliographical tools such as *L'Année Philologique* often failed to include references to many relevant books and articles published by colleagues with similar interests, especially those working in physical education or the history of sports. The fullest published bibliography on ancient sport, that by Egon Maróti (number 98 in this bibliography) is solely concerned with Greek athletics and is not readily accessible to most scholars. Weiler's book (170) on ancient athletics contains a wealth of bibliographical references with sound criticism and discussion, but many citations imbeded in the context of his discussions are not in his bibliographical listings and his author index is not complete. Those without German cannot easily use it as a bibliography. There are increasing numbers of classicists and sports historians in the United States who have become interested in the area of Greek and Roman athletics for research, since it has recently benefited from the new methodologies of the social sciences, and for teaching, since courses on this topic are becoming ever more popular in the universities.

Teachers and students in the fields of classical philology, physical education, art history, sociology, anthropology, psychology, and philosophy will naturally profit from use of this work. But the bibliography is also intended for the use of the autodidactic layman who has an intrinsic interest in things ancient or athletic and who appreciates the enduring significance of sport.

This bibliography has been divided into categories which reflect the trends and interests of past scholarship. Thus one can tell at a glance that there has been a great deal of interest in technical aspects of the Greek events (398 entries), while there has been relatively little in the Roman events (80 entries). I have included some works on games and physical activities which are on the fringe of true sports by our own definitions, i.e. dance, acrobatics, hunting, children's play and board games; most of these appear under "Miscellaneous" headings in Sections VI. M and X. C. Works on games and festivals, the social context of sport, and archaeological evidence and literature pertaining to athletics have also been included. Bibliographical information on each work has sometimes been followed by a notice of "Reviews" which have been listed in the order of the most recent first and with the mention of the year of *L'Année Philologique* in which these reviews were cited. Titles or parts of a title which were originally in Greek script have been transliterated. German umlauts have been resolved into their diphthong form, i.e. the vowel and an "e".

COMMENTARY

The following comments on the categories included in this bibliography are meant to serve merely as an outline of the most significant works in each area and the questions which have been treated. It is intended to be more a guideline to scholarship than a qualitative analysis of the works cited, although some general criticisms are made, the history of scholarship on certain topics is surveyed, and suggestions for new research are offered.

I. GREEK ATHLETICS: GENERAL AND MISCELLANEOUS

The first systematic description of Greek sports was undertaken by Johann Krause (79), who in 1840 criticized the sixteenth century studies of P. Faber (34) for using mainly written sources and of H. Mercurialis (107) for his diatetic approach to athletics. Krause's aim was "genaue Ermittlung der Tatsachen, des factischen Bestandes, welchen das Altertum liefert" (p. xxix).

Julius Bintz (9) in his 1878 work, *Die Gymnastik der Hellenen,* gives a brief, popular overview of the history, sites and events of the panhellenic games. Lorenz Grasberger (49) in 1864-80 wrote a multivolume work on ancient education, including Greek and Roman physical education; this is still quite useful for its detailed treatment of literary sources. Ernst Curtius through his excavations at Olympia (1875-1881) and writings on ancient athletics (325, 326, 327, and 470) paved the way for a greater appreciation of the Greek competitive spirit and for the modern revival of the Olympic Games.

With Julius Juethner's scholarship (65-73, etc.) in the first half of this century came a new phase of sport history which used the newly emerging fields of archaeology, epigraphy, and papyrology. Most notably he produced a valuable edition and commentary of Philostratus' *On Gymnastics* (1516), many *RE* articles, and, his magnum opus, a general two volume survey of the history and the events of Greek athletics edited postumously by F. Brein (65).

Another encyclopedic scholar of archaeology and philology was Emil Reisch (132-136) who contributed many articles to the first volume of *RE*. Among more recent German scholars, O. W. Reinmuth has written many athletics articles in *Der kleine Pauly* (126-131) and Popplow (122) has written a very useful and interesting survey of the history of Greek athletics, one strength of which is its synthesis of the religious, the cultural and the social aspects of Greek sports throughout antiquity.

E. Norman Gardiner remains the most distinguished and lucid English writer on ancient athletics. His first book, *Greek Athletic Sports and Festivals* (41), still the single most useful English book on that topic, made available to the English speaking world much of what had been done by German scholars like Krause, but Gardiner synthesized and carried forth theories on athletic practice for the benefit of all scholarship. His later *Athletics of the Ancient World* (40) is a condensed version of the earlier work with the useful addition of comparisons to modern practice.

H. A. Harris' *Greek Athletes and Athletics* (50) brings many of Gardiner's studies up to date, compares modern techniques to ancient and makes references to more recent archaeological discoveries. His other noteworthy work, *Sport in Greece and Rome* (51), describes the transition from Greek to Roman sport and treats certain Roman sports, including horse racing and leisure activities. The French scholar Marrou's work on ancient education (99 and 100) includes a more modern, though somewhat less in-depth, analysis of the topic covered by Grasberger.

Patrucco's Italian book (118) offers a generally useful survey and discussion of ancient athletic practice, especially valuable for its careful treatment of archaeological evidence and extensive quotation of primary sources.

Huizinga (59) gives a unique and stimulating interpretation of the philosophical reasons why man, especially ancient man, has been devoted to play.

Scanlon (149a) analyses the significance of the terms *agon* and *aethlos* in early Greek literature.

The latest phase of scholarship on ancient athletics is that which seeks to abandon old national and philosophical biases which stood behind and colored many earlier studies on Greek and Roman culture. It can no longer be assumed that there was a "rise and fall" of Greek athletics which accompanied fifth century cultural progress, nor that the Greeks were unique in their agonal spirit. Pleket (220, 276 and 277), using sociological methods, has attacked traditional views on the rise of professionalism and the decline of ideals; Weiler (170, 171, 225, 226, and 227) using evidence from mythical and historical competitions challenges the traditional characterization of the Greeks as the unique agonal people.

S. Miller (111) and R. S. Robinson (141) are the most useful sourcebooks of ancient literature, inscriptions and papyri related to athletics. Robinson offers more interpretation and more footnotes, as well as a greater number of primary sources in translation, whereas Miller's more slender but judicious selection provides consistently better and more literal translations of much of what Robinson has. Many other important sources not in Robinson are added in Miller's collection.

II. THE ORIGIN AND DEVELOPMENT OF GREEK ATHLETICS.

A. Minoan and Mycenaean Athletics.

The questions which have been treated in this area remain controversial. Were the games of the Minoans sacred or secular? How much did the Mycenaeans owe to the Minoans in their practice of sports? What role was played by hero cults and funeral games in the development of Mycenaean athletics? Popplow (195 and 196) has investigated Minoan bull games and Mycenaean chariot racing in funeral games. Ridington's dissertation (198) is an interesting but rather unsystematic attempt to link Minoan and Mycenaean athletics to later Greek tradition. Sakellarkis' essay (199) on Minoan-Mycenaean athletics is more sound but somewhat sketchy and not well documented. Younger's study (203) is the best analysis yet of the styles of bull-leaping as seen in archaeological remains.

II. B. Athletics in Homer and Greek Myth.

Here, as in other historical investigations involving Homer, one is faced with the difficulty of distinguishing between history and legend, and between Bronze Age references and those to the poet's own time. O'Neal (218) and Weiler (227) criticize standard views of the athletic ideals of Homer; the latter author (225 and 226) also defines and categorizes contests in Greek myth. Pleket in a very important article (220) applies sociological methods to characterize sports in the Homeric world in contrast to those of later Greece.

II. C. Athletics in Archaic and Classical Greece.

Articles on professionalism, training, diet, prizes, punishment and ideals are included in this section, since the sixth and fifth centuries were the crucial periods in development of trends in these areas, although the issues are not restricted to these periods of antiquity.

Pleket (276) discusses the classes of games, the significance of prizes, and the nature of athletic ideals in a crucial article on the question of ancient professionalism in sports. Mannings (97) and Matz (264) offer useful but more traditional views on the subject. Young (287a, 287b) challenges the myth of amateuism in early Greek athletics in two very important studies.

The rise of the gymnasium as a central institution of the Greek polis accompanied the rise of the hoplite class in the sixth century, so that this building, its managers and trainers were well established by the fifth century (*Building:* Boetle, 230; Borthwick, 231; Bussemaker, 233; Bussemaker and Fougères, 234; Delorme, 1305; Glass, 1323; Glotz, 248; Goeber, 250; Oehler, 272; Schneider, 283; *Trainers:* Bussmaker, 233; Fourgères, 244; Girard, 245, 246, and 247; Juethner, 253 and 256; Lawińska-Tyszowska, 259; Oehler, 271 and 273; Preisigke, 278; Reisch, 279; Rudolph, 282; Schulthhess, 284; Zucker, 289, *Training programs:* Crowthner, 236; Karouzou, 257; Kornexl, 258; Meinberg, 265, Musiolek, 268; Weinrich, 287. *Diet:* Diem, 237; Eckman, 238; Edelstein, 239; Reisch, 280; Suandeau and Suandeau-Deterne, 285).

II. D. Hellenistic Greek Athletics and the Ephebia.

During the hellenistic age, a college of youths, the *ephebia,* was established at Athens for military, athletic, and intellectual training of the young sons of the elite. This institution, well documented by inscriptions, remained strong into the second century A.D. and became popular in other parts of the Greek world. Pelekides (303) has written the most extensive study of this topic, while Oehler (301 and 302) and Reinmuth (307, 308, and 309) have important articles on the subject.

III. THE ANCIENT OLYMPICS.

A. General and Miscellaneous.

Since the revival of the Olympic Games in 1896, numerous popular books on the history of the ancient Games or some aspect of them have appeared, usually coincident with a modern Olympic year. At least ten such works appeared in German for the 1936 "Nazi" Berlin Olympics (Curtius, 326; Harbott, 349;Harder, 350; Hege and Rodenwaldt, 352; Hilker, 355;

Kempe, 366; Kreutz, 376; Melber and Steeger, 391; Melber, 392; Popp, 419). Although the quality of such books varies, they are usually popular and represent attempts to publicize or capitalize on "Olympicomania". Some of the more recent general books which are of scholarly significance are: Drees, 332; Finley and Pleket, 337; Gardiner, 342; and Yalouris, 445 and 446. Other works in this category which are noteworthy can be further classified according to the aspect of the games which they investigate: *ideals* (Doell, 331; Gerstenberg, 344; Muth, 407 and 408; Diem, 329), *historical and political import* (Buhmann, 322; Curtius, 325; Ebert, 333; Finley and Pleket, 337; Gardiner, 342; Hoenle, 357; Strempel, 431), *religious association* (Gardiner, 341; Kaldis-Henderson, 364; Kempe, 366; Weniger, 440-444), *chronology* (Mommsen, 401; Miller, 461) and *athletes and victor lists* (Belock, 317; Diels, 328; Ebert, 334; Foerster, 338; Koerte, 373; Moretti, 402 and 403; Parandowski, 411; Rutgers, 425).

III. B. Origins.

The various ancient accounts concerning the origins of the Games conflict with one another largely due to a complex tradition stemming from layers of mythical and legendary explanations to support the claims of the two rival cities, Elis and Pisa, for sponsorship of the games. The names of rulers, heroes, or gods who instituted contests and the nature of the games held differ somewhat in the two versions, as does the traditional date of the first games held in honor of Zeus. How and when the games actually began are questions still debated by scholars. Theories center around a sacred or a secular origin, and around speculation on whether the inspiration for the games came initially from funeral games for heroes, from succession struggles, from wedding games, or from leisurely competition. The most recent survey appears in Ulf and Weiler (465). Drees (453) presents the most comprehensive and synthetic answer in his book on the topic, but much of this is speculative and hypothetical. Cornford's chapter (452) in Harrison's *Themis* gives a controversial yet influential view based on the divine kingship of the hero-victor. Rose's essay (464) and Gardiner's book (342, chap. V) serve as a sober balance to Cornford's theory by suggesting the essentially secular nature of the games. Miller's very important article (461) examines the independent testimonia for the date of individual Olympic festivals to support his convincing, general theory that the ancient Olympics took place every four years at the second full moon after the summer solstice. Miller thus throws serious doubt on the chronological arguments of Weniger and others (441,

442, 468) suggesting that the Olympics were a "moveable feast" founded later than the Heraia. Kretchmer (81) argues on linguistic grounds that the Phrygians played a decisive role in the founding of the Olympic Games through their leader, Pelops. Boutros (451) argues for Phoenician inspiration, since those peoples had similar festival games long before the Greeks.

III. C. The Site.

The site of the ancient Olympic Games was rediscovered by R. Chandler in 1766 and excavated by the Germans under the direction of E. Curtius in 1875-1881. The detailed reports of those early excavations are contained in Curtius' and Adler's monumental work (470) with four volumes of text and one of tables and plates. Doerpfeld's two volume work (473) chronicles the later excavations undertaken between 1906 and 1929. The excavations from 1936 to 1942 were undertaken under the patronage of Adolph Hitler following the Berlin Olympics. During the period 1952-1966 the stadium was uncovered while Emil Kunze (485 and 486) with Hans Schleif and later with Alfred Mallwitz led the excavation and publication of findings.

Important major publications of the site after Curtius include the regular reports in *Berichte ueber die Ausgrabungen in Olympia,* eight volumes (1937-1967) and *Olympische Forschungen,* 12 volumes (1944-1979) under the editorial supervision of Kunze and Schleif (486).

The major recent books are H. V. Herrmann's *Olympia* (482) and A. Mallwitz's *Olympia und seine Bauten* (488) both prepared on the occasion of the 1972 Munich Olympics and both reviewing 100 year's scholarship on Olympia. The best single survey of the site in English for the non-specialist is Drees' *Olympia: Gods, Artists, and Athletes* (332), although the translation from the original German edition is flawed.

IV. THE OTHER PANHELLENIC FESTIVALS.
A. General. B. Pythian. C. Isthmian. D. Nemean.

Studies on the Pythian, Isthmian and Nemean Games have generally centered on the victors, the programs and the sites. Much less have been written on the legendary origins of the Pythian Games, second only to the Olympics in panhellenic greatness (Bilinski, 7; Gardiner, 41; Roux, 521; see also J. Fontenrose, *Python: A Study of Delphic Myth and Its Origins.* Berkeley and Los Angeles: Univ. of Ca. Press, 1980, with excellent bibliography). Much less scholarly attention has been paid to the religious and mythical aspects of the Isthmian and Nemean Games (*Isthmian:* Broneer, 532 and 534; Gardiner 41; Reinmuth, 541. *Nemean:* Gardiner, 41; Reinmuth, 558).

More fruitful for all research on panhellenic games have been the studies of the archaeological finds which appear in excavation reports: for Delphi, *Fouilles de Delphes* published by the École française d'Athènes from the nineteenth century to the present; for Isthmia (since 1952) and Nemea (since the mid-1970's) sports by the American School at Athens in *Hesperia.* Isthmian excavations were first directed by O. Broneer who, significantly for sports history, solved the problem of the *hysplex* or starting gate at that stadium (528 and 640). A comprehensive study of the political role of the panhellenic Isthmian Games might profitably be undertaken. S. Miller has led the excavations at Nemea where the most significant athletic find to date has been the uncovering of the fourth century stadium with its tunnel for ceremonial entrances (Miller, 551-557; Romano, 559).

V. A. and B. The Panathenaic Festival and Local Games.

Local games include those patterned on the panhellenic games in program and in the practice of awarding crowns, and they are thus sometimes called isolympian, isopythian, etc., although value prizes were often awarded in addition to the crowns. Numerous other local games, however, simply offered prizes and incidentally provided a livelihood for many non-noble athletes in the fifth century and later. For all such games archaeological monuments and inscriptions have provided the most useful evidence for determining the nature of each contest. Generally until thirty years ago these contests received scant treatment outside of studies on victor lists and programs from scattered epigraphic and literary sources. But progress in excavations has revealed the breadth and complexity of local games and opened for scholars a promising area for future studies on the political, social, economic, and historical import of the games. Ringwood's studies (612-618) have established a basis for further investigation by isolating many of the features of local contests. Some noteworthy studies on the Panathenaea are Davison (562), Thompson (576), and Ziehen (578). Laemmer (600-602) has studied contests in ancient Israel. L. Robert's many epigraphical investigations of local festivals has helped lay the groundwork for any comprehensive study of local festivals (619-626 and 1451-1468).

VI. THE EVENTS.

Research on Greek athletics has been largely concerned with the nature and practice of the events. It has occupied the attention of the field's greatest scholars, each of whose works has marked a significant step forward in understanding the exact ways in which events were played and how they originated. Among the most noteworthy books or monographs are the following: Krause (79 and 80), Grasberger (49), Bintz (9), Juethner and Brein (65), Gardiner (40 and 41), Harris (50 and 51), Ebert (781), and Patrucco (118).

Most of these works are listed under section I, "Greek Athletics: General", since they occur in the context of more general discussions of Greek athletics and they constitute what has occupied a large part of the attention of scholars on ancient athletics until quite recently. Cross-references to the relevant chapters of these books on the events have generally not been included in this bibliography under the headings of each event (Section VI. A-M), so that the user of this work should consult those studies for general discussion of techniques and problems concerning the events. What have been listed here under "Events" are more technical or specialized studies on particular aspects of each event.

VI. A. Running. B. The Torch Race.

Some of the more controversial or significant problems which have been the subjects of studies on running are: *ultra-long-distance running* (Allison, 634; Bilinski, 639; Bussemaker, 642; Diem, 644 and 645; Hueppe, 650; Hyde, 652, Juethner, 657; Lucas, 664; Matthews, 665; Mezö, 667; Suolathi, 684); *starts and lanes* (Broneer, 640; Miller, 668; Reisch, 681; Roos, 683); and *hoplite races* (Beazley, 636; Bilinski, 638; Neumann, 674). The torch race has special scholarly significance, although it was never a part of the Olympic program, since it was one of the few team sports in ancient Greece with teams sometimes determined by tribe (686-695).

VI. C. Jumping.

With regard to jumping, there is still little consensus as to whether the event was a single or a multiple jump, and whether the take-off was from a running or standing position. The use of *halteres* or jumping-weights presents a further difficulty for reconstruction by modern scholars: how were they used and when were they released (Juethner, 705 and 710; Linder, 715 and 716; Reinmuth, 721; de Ridder, 724). But one of the most intriguing scholarly puzzles involves the record jump of Phayllus of Croton, who supposedly leapt an incredible fifty-five feet (Gardiner, 699; Harris, 701; Howland, 702; Juethner, 708; Kueppers, 712; Mezö 717; Stier, 725). This unique statistic has also led (or misled) scholars in their theories on the performance of the jump in normal competition, but there has been yet little agreement.

VI. D. Discus Throwing.

The technique of throwing the discus has been equally problematic. Was it thrown with a spin of the body and, if so, how much of a spin? Motions preliminary to the throw have been postulated on the basis of the depictions on vase painting, and the famous sculpture by Myron, the *Discobolos,* has prompted as much speculation as it has inspired praise for its harmonious proportions (Dihl, 733; Juethner, 742; Schroeder, 750; Sieveking, 753 and 754; Suemeghy, 755 and 756; Uhlig, 758). Scholars have also theorized on the origin of this unusual event (Castiglione, 729), with the latest and most convincing answer from W. Decker (732) who sees the discus originally as the product of an ancient Near Eastern smelting processes.

VI. E. Javelin Throwing.

Problems concerning the javelin have included how far it was thrown, whether the *amentum* or throwing strap was attached or unattached, and from what part of the field it was thrown (Lee, 767).

VI. F. The Pentathlon.

The ancient pentathlon has prompted research mainly in two areas: the method of determining victory, and the order of the events. Theories concerning the methods used to determine victory include a kind of point system (Gardiner, 785; Ebert, 780-781) and a system of the most victories (Harris, 789). The only certainty in the order of events is that wrestling came last. It is disputed whether the footrace was first (Gardiner, 41), or fourth (Harris, 50; Ebert, 781). There is no evidence for the order of discus, javelin, and the jump, the field events unique to the pentathlon.

VI. G. Wrestling. H. Boxing. and I. Pankration.

Scholarship on the popular heavy events, wrestling, boxing, and pankration, centers on discussion of technique and on the famous athletes who practiced the sports. The fullest single treatment of the heavy events is that of Rudolph (424). Discussions of the careers of athletes include not only legendary figures like Milo, Diagoras, Pollux, Amycus, and Glaucus, but also the less famous historical figures known only through a chance inscription or literary reference (Dunst, 815; Mellor, 827; Merkelbach, 828 and 877; Robert, 834, 861, and 882; Ebert, 840). Of some special scholarly interest is the development of types of boxing gloves from the simpler to the more dangerous (Borthwick, 839; Juethner, 843; Mender, 850; Mohler, 853; Reinmuth, 858). Poliakoff (829a) provides a detailed philological study of eight terms pertaining to the heavy events.

VI. J. Greek Equestrian Events.

Among the noteworthy studies on horse and chariot racing are Anderson's authoritative book on horsemanship (885), Harris' studies on the starting gate for chariots at Olympia (893-894) and Reisch's series of *RE* articles on unusual types of horse acrobatics (915-922).

VI. K. Greek Water Sports and Games.

Despite their preoccupation with seafaring and the *thalassios bios,* the Greeks generally did not consider the sea to be the proper place for sporting competition. Nevertheless there were some boat races (Gardner, 566, 935 and 937; Harris, 51; Patrucco, 118). The absence of swimming competition has been an object of concern to several German scholars (Auriga, 932 and 933; Geiss, 938; Mehl, 942-947; Reuel, 950; Schuetze, 953). Was it merely due to lack of suitable waters at the panhellenic sites, absence of a tradition of aquatic sports, or some other reason?

VI. L. Greek Ball Games.

Although Greek ball games were never part of public competition (Hirn, 965; Young, 992), they did play an important role in training and were a favorite leisure activity. The place of ball games in Galen's *On Exercise with the Small Ball* (*Parv.pil.*) has been studied by Heubaum (964) and Nickel (977). An English translation of the work, with notes, is found in Robinson (141). Teams of Spartan ball players are known from inscriptions (Tod, 986-987; Woodward, 991). The variety of Greek ball games is attested by the number of special names (*phaininda, harpastum, episkyros, trigon, keretizontes,* etc.). These are each the subject of special studies in encyclopedic articles.

VI. M. Miscellaneous Greek Events.

Greek competition in archery is known from literature as early as the Funeral Games for Patroclus in *Iliad* 23 and, of course, from the contest of the bow for the suitors in *Odyssey* 21. Nevertheless the event was never incorporated into the program of later festivals (Bérard, 993; Brain and Skinner, 995; Gross, 998; Lambert, 1009; McCartney, 1012; Miltner, 1017; Saglio, 1025; Schaumberg, 1027; Stern, 1030). Nor was hunting considered a competitive sport as such (Butler, 997; Orth, 1020; Tilander, 1031). Greek children's games are the subject of several studies (Brackova, 994; Herter, 999; Hett, 1000; Lambin, 1010; Lefebvre-Verreydt, 1011; Mingazzini, 1018; Schmidt, 1028).

VII. ROMAN ATHLETICS: General.

Until now there has been much more scholarly interest in Greek athletics than Roman. This may be the heritage of eighteenth and nineteenth century attitudes which idolized the Greeks as the forefathers of many ideals of western culture, including the fair-play ethic, and which characterized the Romans as a utilitarian race which only had time for sport as entertainment for the masses. Whatever the truth of these generalizations, they have fostered studies which not only criticize the cruelty and inhumanity of Roman sports, but also question whether such public displays should even be called sports or athletics (Auguet, 1033-1034; Friedlander, 1043; Grant, 1207).

Recently the more enlightened views of Weiler (170) have argued that the stereotypical characterization of Greek and Roman athletics and the consequent disparagement of Roman spectator sports is basically unhistorical. Circuses, gladiatorial battles, and beast games (*ludi circenses, munera gladiatorum, venationes*) which have occupied most of the scholarly attention on this topic were indeed important in the social, political, economic, and religious life of late Republican and Imperial Romans. Are these exhibitions not as deserving of the name sport as the modern displays of professional football, horseracing, and auto racing? Moreover the topics of Roman private games and leisure sports (Vaeterlein, 1071) and popular Roman attitudes to Greek athletics (Maehl, 1056) have received relatively little attention, although it is in these areas that one can most fairly compare Roman attitudes to a play ethic and to personal fitness with the views of the Greeks. Roman athletics were of course to some extent influenced by Greek and Etruscan models. For this reason and in view of the fact that Greek athletics were popular among Roman youths, the often cited Roman aversion to Greek athletics can be attributed largely to the protests of a conservative minority.

In general what seems to be needed for a better appreciation of Roman athletics and physical education is a careful re-evaluation of the unique place which public and private sport occupied in Roman society. Leisure-time exercise in the baths, hunting and ball-playing were as important for the Romans as organized competitions in running and wrestling were for the Greeks. If the public games in Rome served as festival entertainment for the *populus,* it did so in a much different way than the athletic festival of the Greeks. In any case the gross differences between athletics in those two societies ought not to lead to disparagement of this aspect of Roman culture due to comparison with the Greek.

VIII. THE ORIGINS & DEVELOPMENT OF ROMAN ATHLETICS.

A. Etruscan, Early Roman, and Republican Athletics.

Whatever the origins of the Etruscan people, Etruscan athletics, known largely through the artistic evidence, owe much to the Greek in their practices of boxing, wrestling, and discus and javelin throwing, and perhaps even equestrian events (see especially Bronson, 1083; Diem, 1084; Huergon, 1092; Sawula, 1103; Schmidtchen and Howell, 1104). Chariot racing reveals Greek influence in the arrangement of horses and in the technique of driving (Bronson, 1083). The earliest depiction of the *lusus Troiae,* a riding competition among Roman youths, is the Etruscan Oinochoe of Tragliatella (Giglioli, 1088). The most famous description of this exercise in literature comes in Vergil *Aeneid* 5.545ff. during the Funeral Games for Anchises (Diem, 1085; Grothe, 1090; Heller, 1091; Knight, 1096; Schneider, 1105). These games are probably not Greek or Trojan in origin, but Etruscan with possible Near Eastern roots. Gladiatorial contests and beast games also seem to be part of the Roman heritage from Etruria or Campania. The association of Etruscan games mainly with funeral rites, if correct, resembles Greek games only in part, since the Greeks held games for a number of other reason as well (Hus, 1093). In any case, the Etruscans seem to have lacked the competitive zeal for athletics which is more widely evident among the Greeks.

VIII. B. Athletics during the Empire.

The Juvenalian phrase, *panem et circenses,* has long served as a slogan to typify the political indolence and venality of the Roman people, but it can conversely illustrate the importance of games and bread doles as powerful tools of emperors and magistrates. The political and social significance of the games has been the subject of several studies (Cameron, 1115-1117; Deninger, 1120; Goellmann, 1122; Veyne, 1137). The politicization of the games began in the late Republic and became established practice throughout the principate (Bollinger, 1113; Brind'Amour, 1114; Cameron, 1117; Cavallars, 1119; Habel, 1123; Harmon, 1125; Herz, 1126; Langenfeld, 1131; Rudolph, 1135; Ungern-Sternberg, 1136). Physical remains of circuses and amphitheaters at the sites of most larger Roman cities attest to the widespread importance of the institution of games (Gentili, 1121; Juethner, 1127; Krencker, 1128; Lancel, 1129; Ungern-Sternberg, 1136). Even the baths, important centers of exercise and leisure activity, could become political tools (Meusel, 1132). Lee (1131a) discusses the phenomenon of "team" fans in ancient Rome.

IX. ALIEN ATTITUDES TO ATHLETICS: The Greeks, Christians, and Jews under Rome.

Despite the disdain for Greek athletics and culture by some Roman authors, athletic festivals organized in the Greek style were endorsed by the Emperors Augustus, who founded the Actian Games (Briggs, 1499; Gagé, 1150; Reisch, 1171; Varwig, 1177), Nero, who founded the Neronia in A.D. 60 (Varwig, 1178), and Domitian, who founded the Capitoline Games in A.D. 86 (Wissowa, 1181). These games along with the smaller local Greek games sponsored by Romans within and beyond Italy were quite popular among Romans (Arnold, 1138; Bowersock, 1143-1144; Briggs, 1499; Eisenhut, 1149; Gagé, 1150; Geer, 1151; Juethner, 1155; Laemmer, 1160; Maehl, 1056; Meier, 1162; Merkelbach, 1163; Reisch, 1171; Robert, 1172-1173; Robinson, 1174; Tidman, 1175; Varwig, 1177-1179; Wissowa, 1181). Augustus founded the *Iuventus* or "Youth Corps" which had its Greek counterpart in the paramilitary *Ephebia* (Huber, 1154; Ladage, 1159; Mohler, 1165; Pfister, 1168-1169). Romans in the Eastern Mediterranean had often taken over the management of Greek gymnasia and the direction and financing of Greek contests (Robert, 619-626, 1451-1468; Pleket, 306).

The attitudes of early Christians to Greek and Roman athletics were mixed. Greek athletics were accepted insofar as they provided inspiration for the metaphor of winning the *agon* and they served as religious ceremonies or funeral games (Bondolfi, 1142; Gryglewicz, 1152; Kannengiesser, 1156; Ortega, 1166; Pfitzner, 1170). Yet athletics which served primarily as entertainment, and this of course means the Roman circuses, gladiatorial and beast games especially, were criticized by Tertullian and other Church fathers as "the devil's work" (Ebert, 1148; Koch, 1157-1158; Weismann, 1180). Zellinger (1182) illustrates the particular criticism which Christians had for mixed bathing *(balnea mixta)*, although the Romans themselves did not universally endorse this practice (see Carcopino, 1118).

X. THE ROMAN EVENTS.

A. Roman Equestrian Events.

Roman horse and chariot racing seems to have had an Etruscan origin and differed from Greek racing in many particulars (Harris, 51; Balsdon, 1110; Regner, 1134; Nachod, 1192). Etruscan itself may have been influenced by Greek practice earlier. In organization and actual running of the race, in the roles of participants, managers and spectators, and in the sociopolitical function of the circuses, they stand unique and largely independent from the Greek tradition. Inscriptions are particularly useful among source materials for racing terminology, rules, factional divisions, and the prosopography of horses and drivers (Cameron, 1185; Syme, 1197).

X. B. Gladiators and *Venationes.*

The unique Roman institution of gladiatorial contests has given rise to several popular works which can only superificially approach the questions concerning the origin, development, and social function of the games (Auguet, 1033-1034; Grant, 1207; Pearson, 1214). Robert's work, on the other hand, is a model study of gladiators in the Greek Orient, and one carefully drawn chiefly from inscriptional evidence (1215). Many individual studies also treat the funerary inscriptions, painted notices, and relief sculptures of these warriors (Blaźquez-Martinez, 1202; Faccenna, 1203; Frisch, 1204; Matz, 1211; Sabbatini, 1216-1219; Wahl, 1227). More technical and reliable studies on general questions include Toynbee (1224) on the origins, Friedlander (1043), Schneider (1221) and Ville (1226) on development, Amelotti (1200) on the legal position, and Neppi-Modona (1213) on the amphitheaters.

X. C. Miscellaneous Roman Sports.

Ball play was perhaps even more important for Roman personal physical fitness than for Greek, since along with swimming it was incorporated into the routine of exercise in the baths (Balsdon, 1110; Carcopino, 1118; Harris, 51; Mau, 968 and 971; Mendner, 972-973; Mitchell, 976). The actual games were for the most part identical with or similar to those of the Greeks and included *trigon* and *phaininda-harpastum* as well as a kind of volleyball with the *follis* (Mendner, 974; Wegner, 1252; Wilhelm, 1254; Young, 992).

X. D. Roman Aquatic Spots.

The fact that Augustus considered *litterae et natare* as the *rudimenta* of the Roman's education (Suet. *Aug.* 64) suggests the importance of swimming in baths, rivers, or the seas as a part of the daily Roman routine. Yet like the Greeks, the Roman probably never held formal competition in swimming (Harris, 51; Mehl, 942-947; Sanders, 952; Strempel,1260). Competitions in sailing and rowing were not regular, organized events; mock sea-battles, *naumachiae,* on the other hand, were regularly held after the first such spectacles given by Julius Caesar and by Augustus (Balsdon, 1110; Friedlaender, 1043; Harris, 51; Traversari, 1250).

XI. ROMAN BATHS.

The great baths at Rome and in the provinces were important as centers of leisure activity and socializing which provided not only hot and cold pools for swimming and bathing, but also gymnasia, palaestrae, ball-playing areas, and libraries (Mau, 1269; Micca, 1271). Some of the larger baths were built by emperors such as Nero, Titus, Trajan, Diocletian, Caracalla, and Constantine (Meusel, 1132; Cunliffe, 1264; Fine-Licht, 1265; Grunauer, 1266; Krencker, 1267; Krencker et al. 1268). Baths functioned in a capacity similar to that of the palaestra in Greek society as one of the central fixtures of any sizeable city. Yet the Roman institution was generally less exclusive or elitist, and women could and did often attend.

XII. ATHLETICS IN ART AND ARCHAEOLOGY.

A. General.

Since the material evidence for Greek athletics has played such an important part in understanding this area of Greek culture, and since athletic themes constitute so much of ancient art, it is not possible here to do justice to the enormous body of scholarship which relates directly or indirectly to this area. The works treated here are mostly studies dealing exclusively with athletic sculpture, vase painting, and coins, as well as stadia, gymnasia, and palaestrae.

There are, generally speaking, three approaches taken to the material: consideration of objects and sites purely for their value within the fields of classical art history and archaeology, analysis of material evidence mainly for its contribution to our knowledge of ancient athletics, and, thirdly, some combination of the approaches of art history and athletic history. This bibliography is mainly concerned with the latter two approaches, although the standard art handbooks indispensible for much athletic research are also cited here (Beazley, 1276, 1277, 1280; Bieber, 1285; Boardman, 1289-1290; Boethius and Ward-Perkins, 1291; Durm, 1311; Neppi-Modona, 1363).

There are few general works on Greek athletic art (Buschor, 1299; Greco, 1324; Gross, 1325; Harris, 1328; Hyde, 484; Jerace, 1341; Neutsch, 1364; Putnam, 1375; Schroeder, 1384; Vighi, 1395-1396). Of these the most successfully comprehensive is Hyde (484), although this could profit from updating. Legakis in his unpublished dissertation (1348) has done a very thorough evaluation of athletic art in the archaic period.

Many articles discuss specific statues or vases by a certain artist or in a certain museum. Some treat a special class of athletic art, such as Brauchitsch on panathenaic amphorae (1293), Burkhardt on equestrian vase paintings (1298), Gross on victor statues (1325), and Bernhard and Lange on athletic types on coins (1284 and 1347). There are a number of studies on statue bases (Casson, 1301; Della Seta, 1303-1304; Hook, 1334; Philadelphus, 1368-1371).

Stadia, gymnasia, and palaestrae are given general treatment in a number of works (Delorme, 1305; Dorigny, 1308; Fiechter, 1313; Fougères, 1314; Glass, 1323; Harris, 1329; Jerace, 1341; Moestue, 1354-1356; Romano, 1380b; Schneider, 1383; Zschietzschmann, 1404-1405). Fullest and most important of these are Delorme (1305) Glass (1323), and Romano (1380a).

The popularity of Roman public games is evidenced by the proliferation of lamps, reliefs, mosaics, inscriptions, and grafitti whose subjects are gladiators, circuses, and beast games. This artistic evidence has most often been published piece by piece in excavation reports, archaeological journals, and museum catalogues. General treatments of Roman sports are few.

Robert's series of articles on gladiatorial monuments (1377) is one of the few studies exclusively on such art. Illustrations of Roman athletics with minimal discussion can be found in Grant (1207) and Auguet (1033-1034).

Henze (1333) points out that several of Rome's greatest and most unique contributions to architecture are in the realm of "sports architecture:" the circus, the amphitheater, and baths. Standard handbooks on Roman architecture which contain useful discussions of amphitheaters are Bieber (1285), Boethius and Ward-Perkins (1291), Colagrassi (1302), Durm (1311), and Neppi-Modona (1357). Two popular works in English also treat the architecture and spectacles of the Colosseum: Pearson (1214) and Quennell (1376). See Section XI. for works on the architecture of the Roman bath.

XII. B. Inscriptions.

Greek agonistic inscriptions include those set up by victorious athletes or patrons on statue bases or *stelai,* as well as general inscriptions relating to the management and organization of athletic festivals. These inscriptions are of course extremely valuable documents for ancient sports history, since they provide the essential and often the only evidence for certain aspects of the nature of the games, the background of athletes, the titles and duties of organizers and trainers, and many other details. The importance of these documents has been outlined by Laemmer (1426), who sees the primary nature of the inscriptions and the insights gained from new finds as their chief contributions to studies in ancient athletics. Important earlier epigraphical studies include Dittenberger and Purgold (1410), Klee (75), Knab (504), and Ringwood (612). More recently Moretti (402-403, 1437) in two important works has assembled the inscriptional evidence for all known Olympic victors and for other victors in general, arranged into chronological periods of Archaic, Classical and Hellenistic Greek, and Roman Republican and Imperial. Ebert's work (1415) on Greek victory epigrams reviews in detail 81 such inscriptions from the sixth century B.C. onward. Robert has contributed numerous (almost 60 by Laemmer's count) commentaries on individual inscriptions and articles based on inscriptional evidence, many of which are listed in this bibliography under sections I. (140), V. B. (619-626) and XII. B. (1451, 1454, 1456, 1459-1463, 1465, 1468). In general one can also consult the major epigraphical journals for publication of individual inscriptions which pertain to athletics: *Zeitschrift fuer Papyrologie und Epigraphie* (= *ZPE;* Bonn,

1967ff.), *Supplementum Epigraphicum Graecum* (=*SEG;* Leiden, 1923ff.), and *L'année épigraphique* (=*AE;* Paris, 1962ff.).

XIII. ATHLETICS IN LITERATURE.

Useful surveys of ancient literary sources appear in Juethner and Brein (65), and Weiler (170), as well as in the sourcebooks of Robinson (141), Miller, (111) and Berger and Moussat (1522). Of the technical writings on athletics, the most extensive and significant left to us are those of Philostratus, Lucian, and Galen. Juethner's edition (1516) of Philostratus' *On Gymnastics (Perì gymnastikes)* with text, translation, and ample commentary, remains the definitive critical work on this manual of physical training. Noccelli's translation and commentary (1517) updates Juethner. This Philostratus of the second to third century A.D. may or may not be the same as the author of the *Imagines (Eikones),* a series of ecphrastic descriptions of 64 paintings, one of which gives the fullest extant account of a pancration match (Harris, 1513; Juethner, 1515).

The second century A.D. Lucian, a Cynic philosopher and satirist, wrote an imaginary dialogue, *Anacharsis,* between the Athenian Solon and the Scythian Anacharsis on the topic of athletics (Steindl, 1576; Robinson, 141; Jakobinyi, 1548; Wilhelm, 1583). This ancient text is important for its discussion of Greek ideals of athletics in the state as well as interesting incidental mention of gymnastic practice.

Galen of Pergamon, a gladiators' doctor of the second century A.D., commented on athletics from a medical point of view in his works *On Exercise with the Small Ball (Perì toû dià tês smikrâs sphaíras gymnasíou)* (Merker, 975; Nickel, 977), *Thrasýboulos, On Maintaining Health (Hygieinà)* (Fetz, 1504; Frank, 1505), and *Exhortation to the Arts (Protreptikós)* (Goehler, 1506). All of these except *Thrasýboulos* are translated in whole or in part in Robinson's sourcebook (141).

Literature which deals specifically with technical issues of sports was generally a late phenomenon. More commonly references to sports are found throughout Greek and Latin poetry and prose in *loci* of varying importance. Games came to be a standard *topos* in the epic tradition beginning with Homer and continuing with Apollonius Rhodius, Vergil, Statius, Valerius Flaccus, Silius Italicus, Quintus Smyrnaeus, and Nonnus. The tradition of epic games (usually funeral) is documented by Willis (1585). The games in the *Iliad* and *Odyssey* pose the central question of whether they more truly reflect the Homeric or the Heroic Age. In general on this question see Section II. B. How do Homeric spirit and practice follow from an earlier tradition and lead to the age of the athletic festival to come? Vergil's literary epic on the other hand more faithfully reflects Roman sports and sportsmanship of the age of Augustus (Briggs, 1499; Mehl, 1501). Although the third century A.D. Heliodorus's *Aethiopica* is not properly an epic, this prose romance is partly in that tradition and contains a vivid description of a wrestling match (Book 10.31-32) translated in Robinson (141) with further analysis by Diem (1530). Theocritus' twenty second Idyll on the boxing match between Pollux and Amycus falls into a similar tradition derived from epic. Sports metaphors also abound in the Greek epic tradition (Lochner-Huettenbach, 1556-1557).

Xenophanes' poem (Diehl 2) on "The Athlete and the Philosopher" is important as one of the earliest criticisms of athletics (Bowra, 1477). Criticism of athletics continues in later poetry for various motives and with varying degrees of seriousness. It appears in satyr plays (Greifenhagen, 1540; Sutton, 1577), in the Greek epigrams of Lucillius and in the Roman poetry of Juvenal (Dellisanti, 1526; Piernavieja, 1569; Robert 1572).

The victory odes of Pindar, Baccylides and Simonides, on the other hand, represent by the perfection of their form a literary tribute to the athlete equal to the greatness of the tribute in plastic arts by Praxiteles or Myron. These epinician hymns are of limited yet significant help in the technical questions of athletic style, victory lists, status of trainers, and festival programs. More obviously the odes embody the spirit of excellence in fifth century athletics which cannot be conveyed otherwise in prose. A number of scholars have, however, analysed the historical elements behind the myth and art of Pindar in order to answer more technical questions. Kramer's study (1483) is the fullest such essay including chapters on the Pindaric victor-list, Greek contests in Pindar's time, the trainers in Pindar, and Heracles as model of the athlete. Woloch (1489) also examines certain trainers mentioned in victory odes, and Wuest (1490) looks at victory lists. Lee (767) uses the evidence of the odes for details of javelin throwing.

Philosophers, historians, orators, and other prose writers often comment on athletics as an essential part of the education and maintenance of the people. The role of athletics in society was a question which occupied Plato, especially in the *Republic* Books III, IV and V on education, but also in the *Laws* and the *Gorgias*. The latest attempt to understand Plato's unusual athletic program, which included athletics for women and generally resembled the Spartan system, is by Meinburg (265).

I have included articles on papyrological texts concerning athletics in the section on literary sources, although these are more documents than literature *per se*: the fragment of a wrestling manual (Cazzaniga, 1525, see 814); Herminus-Moros' cetificate of membership in an athletic guild (Gerstiner, 1536; Wilcken 1581); benefits for athletes' families (Wilcken 1582); and payment of pension (Wilcken 1582).

In addition to the sourcebooks of Robinson (141) and Miller (111) already mentioned, there are a few other collections of source material, some with special definition. Berger and Moussat (1522) is a general collection in French. Kopp's is restricted to early Greek poetry (1551). Welskopf (1579) discusses the question of professionalism as reflected in fifth and fourth century literature and philosophy. Piernavieja del Pozo (1568) lists references to athletics in Latin literature with passages from Cicero, Catullus, Vergil, Horace, Tibullus, Propertius, Ovid, Seneca, Martial, and Gellius.

XIV. ATHLETICS: Other Ancient and Modern Societies.

Recent scholarship in sports history under the influence of the social sciences has placed an increasing importance on viewing Greek and Roman athletics in a cross-cultural context, in relation to that of modern and of other ancient and primitive societies. Wieler (170-171) has been the most successful proponent of such a cross-cultural approach by seeking to demonstrate the fallacy in the stereotype of the Greeks as the greatest agonistic race. Pleket (220) has applied the methodologies of the social sciences to show how there was not a straight line of degeneration in Greek athletics from the Homeric hero-athlete to the Hellenistic "professional." Lukas (94) has investigated the universality and uniqueness of sports among the ancient culture of Egypt, Greece, Babylon, and Persia, India, China, and Japan. Diem (1591-1592) has done similar comparative studies with the inclusion of modern societies.

I

GREEK ATHLETICS

General and Miscellaneous

1. ***Alexander, Ch.*** *Greek Athletics.* N. Y.: Metropolitan Museum, 1933.[2]
2. ***Arieti, J. A.*** "Nudity in Greek Athletics." *CW* 68 (1975): 431-436.
3. ***Arnaiz, Zarandona S.*** *El Deporte en Grecia.* Madrid: Ed. del Marimiento, 1964.

   Review: AP 1966: *EClás 10 (1966): 237 Martínez Fresneda.*
4. ***Assa, J.*** "La mujer y el deporte en la antiguedad." *CAF* 5 (1963): 429 ff.
5. ***Basiades, C. H.*** *De veterum Graecorum gymnastice.* Diss: Berlin, 1858.
6. ***Bengston, H.*** "Agonistik und Politik im alten Griechenland." *Kleine Schriften zur Alten Geschichte.* Munich, 1973: 190-207.
7. ***Biliński, B.*** *Agoni ginnici. Componenti artistiche ed intellettuali nell'antica agonistica greca.* Accad. Polacca delle Sc. Bibl. e Centro di Studi a Roma Conferenze 75. Wroclaw: Ossolineum, 1979.

   Review: *NRS* 64 (1980): 460-461 Criniti.
8. ***Biliński, B.*** *L'agonistica sportiva nella Grecia antica. Aspetti sociale e ispirazioni letterarie.* Rome: Signorelli, 1961.

   Reviews: AP 1964: *Mnemosyne* 17 (1964): 207 van der Veer. AP 1963: *RBPh* 41 (1963): 1354-1355 Verdin. AP 1962: *RSC* 9 (1961): 342. *CR* 12 (1962): 91-92 Harris. *AAHG* 15 (1962): 92 Schir. *REA* 3 (1962): 195-196 Delebecque. AP 1961: *GIF* 14 (1961): 185 Pepe. *RCCM* 3 (1961): 422 Brugnoli.
9. ***Bintz, J.*** *Die Gymnastik der Hellenen.* Guetersloh, 1878.
10. ***Bloch, R.*** "Réflexions sur les sports dans la Grèce antique." *Hommages à Marcel Renard.* Bibauw, J., ed. Coll. Latomus 101, 102, & 103; Bruxelles: 60 rue Colonel Chaltin, 1969: vol. 2, 105-112.
11. ***Bloch, R.*** "Les sports dans l'antiquité." *Diogène* 94 (1976): 67-91.
12. ***Bluemel, C.*** *Sport der Hellenen. Ausstellung griechischer Bildwerke.* Berlin, 1936.
13. ***Bogeng, G. A. E.***, ed. *Geschichte des Sports aller Voelker und Zeiten.* 2 vols. Leipzig, 1926.

14. ***Bóhn, F.***, "A testnevelés törtenéte." ("The History of Physical Education") *Testnevelés* 14 (1941): 89-108, 181-210, 285-306, 419-430, 467-481.

15. ***Bóhn, F.*** "A görög gimnasztika Rómában." ("Greek Gymnastics in Rome") *Tornaueag* 29 (1911): 79-82.

16. ***Bónis, É.*** "Egy pannóniai atléta hagyatéka." ("The Legacy of an Athlete from Pannonia.") *Élet és Tudomány* 29 (1974): 898-902.

17. ***Brelich, A.*** *Guere, agoni e culti nella Grecia arcaica.* See no. 205.

18. ***Burkhardt, J.*** *Griechische Kulturgeschichte.* (trans. into Ital. by M. Attardo Magrini.) Florence, 1955: 89-123 (Der agonale Mensch. Die Gymnastik. Olympia).

19. ***Bussemaker*** and ***Saglio, E.*** "Athleta." *D.-S.* 1, 1, Paris, 1877: 515-521.

20. ***Casson, L.*** "A Passion for the Hard Workout." *Horizon* 18, 2 (1976): 12-15.

21. ***De Marchi, A.*** *Gli Elleni nelle istituzioni e nel costume nell'arte e nel pensiero.* Milan, 1924.[2]

22. ***Diem, C.*** *Gedanken zur Sportgeschichte.* Schorndorf, 1963. Beitraege zur Lehre und Forschung der Leibeserziehung 22.

23. ***Diem, C.*** "Sport im alten Hellas." *Olympische Flamme* 2: 527-549.

24. ***Diem, C.*** *Weltgeschichte des Sports und Leibeserziehung.* Stuttgart, 1960.

25. ***Eckstein, F.*** "Athletenhauben." *MDAI(R)* 63 (1956): 90-95.

26. ***Egger, E.*** and ***Fournier, E.*** "Corona." *D.-S.* 1, 2. Paris, 1887: 1520-1537.

27. ***Egger, J. B.*** *Begriff der Gymnastik bei den alten Philosophen und Medizinern.* Diss.: Freiburg, Switzerland, 1903.

28. ***Eisen, G.*** *Sports and Women in Antiquity.* Unpublished M. A. Thesis, U. Mass., Amherst, 1976.

29. ***Eisen, G.*** "The Role of Women in Ancient Fertility Cults and the Origin of Sport." *NASSH* Proc. (1976): 7.

30. ***Elend, S.*** "Leibeserziehung im Geschichtsbild Spartas." *LKE* 62 (1943): 4-8.

31. ***Englert, L.*** "Die Gymnastik und Agonistik der Griechen als politischen Leibeserziehung." *Das neue Bild der Antike.* Berve, H., ed. Vol. I: Hellas. Leipzig, 1942: 218-236.

32. ***Erdey, F.*** "Néháy lap áz ókori sport történetéböl." ("A Few Pages from the History of Ancient Sport.") *Testnevelés* 4 (1931): 550-567, 735-743, 831-839, 959-962. 5 (1932): 48-54.

33. *Ewer, L.* *Die Leibesuebungen und Wettspiele in Altgriechenland und Rom, zugleich Aufklaerung ueber die Olympische Spiele.* Berlin, 1896.

34. ***Faber, P.*** *Agonisticon, sive de re athletica ludisque veterum gymnicis, musicis atque circensibus specilegiorum tractatus. Lugduni, 1592.*

35. ***Farkas, M.*** "A régi Hellas és a Sport (Beta Ottomar)." ("Ancient Hellas and Sport.") *Herkules* 2 (1885): 9. *sz.* 4-5.

36. ***Forbes, C. A.*** "Accidents and Fatalities in Greek Athletics." *Classical Studies in Honor of W. A. Oldfather.* Urbana: Univ. of Illinois Press, 1943: 50-59.

37. ***Forbes, C. A.*** *Greek Physical Education.* New York: AMS Pr., 1970. (repr. of 1929 ed.).

38. ***Gaertringen, F. H. von.*** "Errhephoroi." *RE* 6, 1. Stuttgart, 1907: coll. 549-551.

39. ***Ganszyniec, R.*** "Kranz." *RE* 11, 2. Stuttgart, 1922: coll. 1588-1607.

40. ***Gardiner, E. N.*** *Athletics of the Ancient World.* Oxford: Clarendon Press, 1930, repr. Chicago: Ares, 1979.

Review: AP 1932: *CW* 25 (1932): 175 Fraser, *Gnomon* 1932: 596-603 Juethner.

41. ***Gardiner E. N.*** *Greek Athletics Sports and Festivals.* Dubuque, Iowa: Brown Reprint, 1970 reprint of London: MacMillan, 1910.

42. ***Gassowska, B.*** *Jouets grecs et romains* (in Polish). Warsaw: Museum Narod., 1960.

43. ***Gedda, L.*** *Lo Sport.* Milan, 1931.

44. ***Giglioli, C. Q.*** "Phyllobolia." *Archeologia Classica* 2 (1950): 31-45.

45. ***Gillet, B.*** *Histoire du sport. Paris, 1949. (Que sais-je? 337.).*

46. ***Girard, P.*** "Educatio." *D.-S.* 2, 1. Paris, 1892: 462-477.

47. ***Girard, P.*** *L'éducation athénienne.* Paris, 1891.[2]

48. ***Gostkowski, R.*** *Le sport dans l'antiquité.* (in Polish) Vade mecum, Bibl. klas. Warsaw: PZWS, 1959.

49. ***Grasberger, L.*** *Erziehung und Unterricht im klassischen Altertum.* Wuerzburg, 1864-1880. repr. 3 vols. Aalen: Scientia Verlag, 19, 1971.

50. ***Harris, H. A.*** *Greek Athletes and Athletics.* London: Hutchinson, 1964, and Bloomington: University of Indiana Press, 1966.

Reviews: AP 1968: *AJPh* 89 (1968): 508-510 Fontenrose. AP 1967: *CB* 43 (1967): 94 Boian. *CR* 17 (1967): 381-383 Howland. *CPh* 62 (1967): 269-270 Anderson. *Archaeology* 20 (1967): 324 Wiseman. AP 1966: *CW* 59 (1966): 195 Ridington.

51. ***Harris, H. A.*** *Sport in Greece and Rome.* Aspects of Greek & Roman Life. Ithaca, N. Y.: Cornell University Press, 1972.

Reviews: AP 1976: *CPh* 71 (1976): 289-290 Anderson. *ACR* 3 (1973): 192-193 Harvey. AP 1975: *CR* 25 (1975): 75-77 Richmond. *JHS* 95 (1975): 236-238 Vickers. AP 1974: *AJPh* 95 (1974): 413-414. MacKendrick. AP 1973: *TLS* 71 (1972): 1564. *Phoenix* 27 (1973): 313-314 Baldwin. *AHR* 78 (1973): 1024-1025 Huzar. *Antiquity* 47 (1973): 84-85 Howland. *G&R* 20 (1973): 209 Walcot. *CW* 67 (1973): 183-184 Rexine. *HAnt* 2 (1972): 240-242 del Castillo.

52. ***Heubaum, R.*** "Das hellenische-roemische Bildungsideal und die koerperliche Erziehung." *HfL* 10 (1931): 221-225.

53. ***Hirn, A.*** "Aktualismus, eine neue Methode zur Erforschung der griechischen Leibesuebungen." *HfL* 8 (1928): Nr. 1: 4-6. Nr. 2: 3-4. Nr. 3: 3-5.

54. ***Hirn, A.*** "Die Athletik im Altertum." *Athletik, ein Handbuch der lebenswichtigen Leibesuebungen.* Munich, 1930: 3-27.

55. ***Hirn, A.*** *Ursprung und Wesen des Sports.* Berlin, 1936.

56. ***Hoffman, F.*** *De athletis veterum, eorum diaeta et habitu.* Med. Diss.: Halle, 1717.

57. ***Hornvansky, Gy.*** *Temetési versenyküzdelmek az ösgörögöknél. (Funeral Games in Ancient Greece.)* Budapest, 1900.

58. ***Hueppe, W.*** "Az ó-kori s a modern athletica." *Herkules* 1 (1884) 29. sz.: 7-8. ("A Deutsche Turn-Zeitung f. évi októberi számából") 32. sz. 7.

59. ***Huizinga, J.*** *Homo ludens, essai sur la fonction sociale du jeu.* Paris: Galimard, 1951. English translation (in part by the author): *Homo Ludens: a Study of the Play-element in Culture.* Boston: Beacon, 1955.

Reviews: AP 1952: *RPhilos* 142 (1952): 566 Schuhl. *AIHS* 5 (1952): 388 Putman.

60. ***Jaeger, O. H.*** *Die Gymnastik der Hellenen.* Stuttgart,[2] 1881.

61. ***Jaeger, W.*** *Paideia: The Ideals of Greek Culture.* trans. by Gilbert Highet. 3 vols. N. Y.: Oxford University Press, vol. 1, 1945;[2] vol. 2, 1943; vol. 3, 1944.

62. ***Jahn, R.***, ed. *Zur Weltgeschichte der Leibesuebungen. Festgabe fuer E. Mehl zum 70. Geburtstag.* Frankfurt: W. Limpert, 1960: Index to the writings of E. Mehl. Appendix 1, pages 197-212. Also contains selected articles by Mehl from four decades.

63. ***James, Darlene Z.*** "Sport: A Myth about Consciousness." *Quest* 30 (1978): 28-35.

64. ***Jeux dans l'antiquite. DossArch*** 1980 no. 45.

65. ***Juethner, J.*** *Die Athletischen Leibesuebungen der Griechen I: Geschichte der Leibesuebungen.* Brien, F., ed. *SAWW* 299, 1. Vienna: Boehlau, 1965.

Reviews: AP 1968: *Gnomon* 40 (1968): 376-380 Neuhausen. AP 1967: *CR* 17 (1967): 379-381 Harris. *LEC* 35 (1967): 298 Dumont. AP 1966: *REA* 68 (1966): 453 Marcadé. AP 1971: *AJA* 75 (1971): 102-103 Broneer.

66. ***Juethner, J.*** "Herkunft und Grundlagen der griechischen Nationalspiele." *Die Antike* 15 (1939): 231-264.

67. ***Juethner, J.*** *"Kónis."* *RE* 11, 2. Stuttgart, 1922: coll. 1312-1315.

68. ***Juethner, J.*** *Koerperkultur im Altertum.* Jena, 1928.

69. ***Juethner, J.*** "Professionalismus im Altertum." *Die Leibesuebungen* 3 (1927): 114-118.

70. ***Juethner, J.*** "Siegerkranz und Siegerbinde." *Oesterr. Jahresh.* 1 (1898): 42-48.

71. ***Juethner, J.*** *Ueber antike Turngeraethe.* Vienna, 1896.

72. ***Juethner, J.*** "Zur Geschichte der griechischen Wettkaempfe." *WS* 53 (1935): 68-79.

73. ***Juethner, J.*** "Zur Namensgebung einst und jetzt: Gymnastik, Athletik, Koerperspiel." *Die Leibesuebungen* 8 (1932); 441-445.

74. ***Jung, A.*** *Massage und Sport im Altertum und Gegenwart.* Diss.: Bonn, Kubens, 1930.

75. ***Klee, Th.*** *Zur Geschichte der gymnischen Agone an griechischen Festen.* Leipzig-Berlin: B. G. Teubner, 1918.

76. ***Klincsek, K.*** "A hellén nök testgyakorlata." ("Physical Exercise of Greek Women.") *Tornaügy* 5 (1887-88): 86-89.

77. ***Koerbs, W.*** "Interpretationsansaetze der antiken Gymnastik und Agonistik." *Dt. Sporthochschule Koeln, Fachtagung* 15.-17. Dec., 1967. Cologne, 1968: 1-11.

78. ***Koerbs, W.*** "Kultische Wurzel und fruehe Entwicklung des Sports." *Studium Generale* 13 (1960): 11-21.

79. ***Krause, J. H.*** *Die Gymnastik und Agonistik der Hellenen* (= idem, *Hellenica* vols. 1-2). Leipzig, 1841, reprinted Wiesbaden: Martin Saendig, 1971 with intro. by M. Laemmer.

80. ***Krause, J. H.*** *Theagenes, oder wissenschaftliche Darstellung der Gymnastik, Agonistik und Festspiele der Hellenen.* Halle, 1835; Hildesheim-N. Y.: Olms, 1975 repr.

81. ***Kretschmer, P.*** "Die phrygische Episode in der Geschichte von Hellas." *Miscellanea Academica Berolinensia* (1950): 173ff. The Phrygians on linguistic grounds played a decisive role in founding the Olympic games through Pelops.

82. ***Kuchenmueller, W.*** "Ho agon kaì tò nóemá tou eis toùs Héllenas. *Platon* 22 (1970) Nos 43-44: 233-240.
83. ***Kun, L.*** *A sport története (The History of Sport.) I.* Budapest, 1966.
84. ***Kun, L.*** *A sport története (The History of Sport.) I. 2. javított kiadás.* Budapest, 1972.
85. ***Kun, L.*** *Egyetemes testnevelés-és sporttörténet. (World History of Sport and Physical Education.)* Budapest, 1978.
86. ***Lamer, H.*** "Theagenes 2." *RE* 6 A, 1. Stuttgart, 1936: coll. 252-257.
87. ***Lawinska-Tyszowska, J.*** "Rol' trenera v drevnej Grecii." *Acta Conventus* 10 (11) *'Eirene.'* Bratislava, 1971: 55-61.
88. ***Lázar, I.*** "A görök testi nevelése." ("The Education of the Body in Greece.") *Herkules* 10 (1943): 190.
89. ***Legakis, B.*** and ***Kilby, L.*** "Journal Survey. New Titles. Antiquity." *JSH* 7 (1980): 64-81.
90. ***Lerche, N.*** "Gymnastik." *KP* 2 (1967): 887-892.
91. ***Loebker, G.*** *Charakter und Bestimmung der Gymnastik in Athen.* Muenster, 1864.
92. ***Loebker, G.*** *Die Gymnastik der Hellenen.* Muenster, 1835.
93. ***Lucas, H.*** "Athletentypen." *JDAI* 19 (1904): 127-136.
94. ***Lukas, G.*** *Die Koerperkultur in fruehen Epochen der Menschheitsentwicklung.* Berlin: Sportverl., 1969.
95. ***Luther, W.*** "Die griechische Gymnastik als Leitbild fuer Sport und Spiel im Gymnasium der Gegenwart." *Studium Generale* 13 (1960): 85-95.
96. ***Macco, G. di.*** "La mujer el deporte a traves de los tiempos." *CAF* 5 (1963): 455ff.
97. ***Mannings, C. A.*** "Professionalism in Greek Athletics." *CW* 11 (1917): 74-78.
98. ***Maróti, E.*** *Bibliographie zum antiken Sport und Agonistik.* Acta Universitatis de Attilla József nominatae. Acta Antiqua et Archaeologica, 22, Szeged, Hungary: 1980.
99. ***Marrou, H. I.*** *A History of Education in Antiquity.* New York and London: Sheed and Ward, 1956.
100. ***Marrou, H. I.*** *Histoire de l'éducation dans l'antiquité.* (trans. into Ital. by U. Massi.) Rome, 1964.
101. ***Méautis, G.*** "Sports antiques et sports modernes." *Conf. à la Soc. des Ét. de Lettres, Lausanne BELL* 26 (1935): 21-24.
102. ***Mehl, E.*** *Grundriss einer Weltgeschichte der Leibesuebungen.* Vortragsreihe Sporthochschule Koeln. Cologne, 1955.
103. ***Mehl, E.*** "Hieronymus Mercurialis, ein alter Streiter fuer die Leibesuebungen." *Die Leibesuebungen* 6 (1930): 561-570.

104. *Mehl, E.* "Leibesuebungen im Altertum." *Stadion. Das Buch von Sport und Turnen, Gymnastik und Spiel.* Diem, C., ed. Berlin, 1928: 29-35.

105. *Mehl, E.* "Turnkunst." *RE* A, 2. Stuttgart, 1948: 2513-2556.

106. *Mehl, E.* "Zur Geschichte des Begriffs Gymnastik." *Festgabe Mehl,* Anhang 22-47, reedited 1960 from *HfL Berlin* (1930): 57-66. See Jahn, R., ed. *Zur Weltgeschichte Leibesuebungen,* no. 62.

107. **Mercurialis, H.** *De arte gymnastica libri 6.* Venice, 1573.

108. *Meuli, K.* *Der griechische Agon. Kampf und Kampfspiel im Totenbrauch, Totentanz, Totenklage und Totenlob.* Cologne, 1968. See no. 215.

109. *Mezö, F.* *A görög sport. (Greek Sport.)* 2 vols. Budapest, 1925-26.

110. *Mezö, F.* *Egyetemus sporttörténelem. (World History of Sport.)* Komárom, 1939 (?). Szerkesztette --.

111. *Miller, S. G.* *Arete. Ancient Writers, Papyri, and Inscriptions on the History and Ideals of Greek Athletics and Games.* Chicago: Ares, 1979.
Review: *JSH* 7 (1980): 92-93 Legakis.

112. *Moerth, O.* "Inwieweit koennen die gymnastischen Uebungen bei den Griechen als soziales Bildungsmittel betrachtet werden?" *ASKO Monatschrift fuer Sport und Koerperkultur.* Vienna, 1950: 5-6.

113. **Mosso, A.** *Mens sana in corpore sano.* Milan, 1903.

114. *Nebel, G.* "Die griechische Athletik." *Antaios* 11 (1960): 189-203.

115. *Oehler, J.* "Gymnastik." *RE* 7, 2. Stuttgart, 1912: 2030-2086.

116. *Oroszlan, Z.* *A görög sport hatása a müvészetekre. (The Influence of Greek Sport on the Arts.)* Budapest, 1948.

117. *Patrucco, R.* "La psicologia dell'atleta." *Maia* 23 (1971): 245-253.

118. *Patrucco, R.* *Lo sport nella Grecia antica.* Arte e archaeol.: Studi e docum. 1. Florence: Olschki, 1972.
Reviews: AP 1975: *ACR* 3 (1973): 93 Segal. AP 1974: *BBF* 19 (1974): 554-555 Ernst. *Athenaeum* 51 (1973): 438-440 Tarditi. AP 1973: *Vet Chr* 10 (1973): 421 Salvatore.

119. *Paulinès, E.* *Historía tes gymnastikes.* Athens, 1953.

120. *Petersen, Ch.* *Das Gymnasium der Griechen nach seiner baulichen Einrichtung.* Hamburg, 1858.

121. *Popplow, U.* "Aufgabe und Sinn einer Urgeschichte der Leibesuebungen." *Die Leibeserziehung* 35 (1959): 309-314, 353-358, 383-390.

122. ***Popplow, U.*** *Leibesuebungen und Leibeserziehung in der griechischen Antike.* Beitr. zur Lehre & Forsch. der Leibeserziehung 2. Schorndorf bei Stuttgart: Hofmann, 1960.

123. ***Porzsolt, J.*** "Az ó-kori és modern athléták." ("Ancient and Modern Athletes.") *Herkules* 4 (1887): 9. sz. 1-.

124. ***Porszolt, L.*** "Professzionisták a régi görögöknél." ("Professional Athletes in Ancient Greece.") *Sport-Világ* 1 (1854): 134ff.

125. ***Raubitschek, A. E.*** "Zum Ursprung und Wesen der Agonistik." *Studien zur antiken Sozialgeschichte. Festschrift F. Vittinghoff.* Eck, W.; Galsterer, H.; Wolff, H., eds. Koelner historische Abhandlungen. Cologne, Vienna, Boehlau, 1980.

125a. ***Raubitschek, A. E.,*** "The Agonistic Spirit in Greek Culture." *AncW* 7 (1983): 3-7.

126. ***Reinmuth, O. W.*** *"Athlon."* *KP* 1 (1964): 706-707.

127. ***Reinmuth, O. W.*** *"Agonothetes."* *KP* 1 (1964): 140-141.

128. ***Reinmuth, O. W.*** *"Athlothétes."* *KP* 1 (1964): 707.

129. ***Reinmuth, O. W.*** *"Braseĩon, Brasentés."* *KP* 1 (1964): 938.

130. ***Reinmuth, O. W.*** *"Hellenodikai."* *KP* 2 (1967): 1006.

131. ***Reinmuth, O. W.*** *"Konis."* *KP* 3 (1969): 292.

132. ***Reisch, E.*** *"Agéneioi."* *RE* 1, 1. Stuttgart, 1894: 722-723.

133. ***Reisch, E.*** *"Agones."* *RE* 1, 1. Stuttgart, 1893: coll. 836-866.

134. ***Reisch, E.*** *"Agonothetes."* *RE* 1, 1. Stuttgart, 1894: 870-877.

135. ***Reisch, E.*** *"Athletai."* *RE* 2, 2. Stuttgart, 1896: coll. 2049-2058.

136. ***Reisch, E.*** *"Athlon."* *RE* 2, 2. Stuttgart, 1896: 2058-2063.

137. ***Renson, R., de Nayer, P. P.,*** and ***Ostin, M.,*** eds. *The History, the Evolution and Diffusion of Sports and Games in Different Cultures. Proceedings of the 4th International HISPA Seminar.* Brussels, 1976.
Review: AP 1978: *Stadion* 3 (1977): 177-180 Weiler.

138. ***Richter, W.*** *Die Spiele der Griechen und Roemer.* Leipzig, 1887.

139. ***Richter, W.*** and ***Takács, M.*** *A görögök es rómaiak játékai. (Games of the Greeks and Romans.) (Átdolgozta Takács Menyhért).* Kassa, 1894.

140. ***Robert, L.*** "Epigraphie greque et géographie historique du monde hellénique (sur la vie agonistique, gymnastique, épique.)" *AEHE 4e Sect.* (1974-1975): 343-350.

141. ***Robinson, R. S.*** *Sources for the History of Greek Athletics in English Translation.* Chicago: Ares, 1979 (reprint of 1955 edition.) With introduction, notes, bibliography, and indices. A revised edition of *The History of Greek Athletics* (1927).

142. *Rohde, E.* *Psyche* (trans. into Ital. by E. Codignola and A. Oberdorfer.) Bari, 1914-1916.

142a. *Roller, L. E.*, "Funeral Games for Historical Persons", *Stadion* 7 (1981) 1-18.

143. *Rose, H. J.* "Greek Agones." *Aberystwyth Studies* 3 (1922): 1-24, Univ. Col., Wales.

144. *Ruby J.* *A hellen gymnastica.* Eperjes, 1877.

145. *Rudolph, W.* "Antike Sportgeraete." *Klio* 48 (1967): 81-92.

146. *Sakellarios, P. G.* "He arkhaîa hellenikè athletike kaì gymnastikè horologìa (Athletikè. Agonistikè. Gymnastiké.)" *PAA* 32 (1957): 232-242.

147. *Sanin, Ju. V.* *Les héros des stades antiques.* (in Russian). Moscow: Fizkultura i sport, 1979.

148. *Saurbier, B.* *Geschichte der Leibesuebungen.* Frankfurt am M., 1954. (1968^{5}).

149. *Saurbier, B.* and *Stahr, E.* *Geschichte der Leibesuebungen.* Leipzig: Voigtlaender, 1939. (Greek and Roman athletics, pp. 11-39.)

149a. *Scanlon, T. F.*, "The Vocabulary of Competition: *Agon* and *Aethlos,* Greek Terms for Contest", *Arete* 1 (1983) 147-162.

150. *Schroeder, B.* "Beitraege zur griechischen Agonistik." *AA* 1925: 203-219.

151. *Schroeder, B.* *Der Sport im Altertum.* Berlin, 1927.

152. *Schroeder, B.* "Orandum est, ut sit mens sana in corpore sano." *Die Leibeserziehung* 1966: 278-281.

153. *Servadio, E.* "Sport." *Enc. It.* 32. Rome, 1936: 415-416.

154. *Stiebitz, F.* "La gymnastique et le sport dans l'antiquité." (in Czech.) Prague: Orbis, 1937.
Review: AP 1940-41: *LF* 65 (1938): 416 Salac.

155. *Strohmaier, G.* ed. "Antike Randnotizen zum Sport." *Altertum* 22 (1976): 27-28.

156. *Szastynska-Siemion, A.* "Le *ponos* du sportif dans l'epinice grec." *Acta Conventus* 10 (11) *Eirene,* 21-25 Oct., 1968. Warsaw: Ossolineum, 1971: 81-85.

157. *Szemzö, L.* *A. testgyakorlás története. (The History of Physical Education.)* Budapest, 1902.

158. *Szemö, L.* "A görög gimnasztika eredete, értéke, oka és helyisége." ("The Origins, Significance, Rationale, and Place of Greek Gymnastics.") *Herkules* 19 (1902): 75-77, 87, 97-99, 115-116.

159. *Thompson, J. G.* *Sport, Athletics, and Gymnastics in Ancient Greece.* Diss. Pennsylvania State Univ.: University Park, 1971. Cf. summary in *DA* 32 (1971): 2584A.

160. *Tod, M. N.* "Greek Record-keeping and Record-breaking." *CQ* 43 (1949): 105-112.

161. ***Turner, E. G.*** and ***Neugebauer, O.*** "Gymnasium Debts and New Moons." *BRL* 32 (1949): 80-96.

162. ***Ueberhorst, H.***, ed. *Geschichte der Leibesuebungen.* 2 vols. Vienna: Bartels & Wernitz, vol. 1: 1972; vol. 2: 1978.
Review: *JSH* 1 (1974): 164-166 Harris.

163. ***Ueberhorst, H.*** "Totenkult und Agone der Griechen." *Sport-medizin* 1 (1950): 176-181.

164. ***Valletti, F.*** *La ginnastica in Roma.* Studi Storici. Palermo, 1884.

165. ***Varady, K.*** "A régi görög versenyek." ("Ancient Greek Contests.") *Herkules* 11 (1894): 120-121.

166. ***Vogt, E.*** "Agon(es)." *KP* 1 (1964): 135-140.

167. ***Vogt, M.*** *Der Antike Sport. Seine Geschichte und Technik.* Tusculum-Schr. 17, Munich: Heimeran, 1934.

168. ***Vogt, M.*** "Der Sport im Altertum." in: Bogeng, A. E. *Geschichte des Sports aller Voelker und Zeiten.* vol. I: 118-162. Leipzig, 1926.

169. ***Wágner, J.*** *Ó-görög sportélet. (Sporting Life in Ancient Greece.)* (Diss: Budapest.) Pápa, 1904.

170. ***Weiler, I.*** *Der Sport bei den Voelker der alten Welt. Eine Einfuehrung.* mit dem Beitrag "Sport bei den Naturvoelkern" von Christoph Ulf. Darmstadt: Wiss. Buchgesellschaft, 1981.

171. ***Weiler, I.*** "Der Wettkampf - ein Privileg der Griechen?" *Historisch-vergleichende Betrachtung. Wort im Gebirge* 15. Innsbruck, 1976: 40-54.

172. ***Wickenhagen, H.*** *Antike und moderne Gymnastik.* Vienna, 1891.

173. ***Wikarjak, M.*** "De arte gymnastica apud Graecos antiquos." (in Polish with Latin summary) *Meander* 15 (1960): 446-455.

174. ***Wilhelm, A.*** "Siegerlisten aus Athen." *MDAI(A)* 30 (1905): 213-219.

175. ***Woody, Th.*** "Professionalism and the Decay of Greek Athletics." *School and Society* 47 (1938): 521-528.

176. ***Wright, F. A.*** *Greek Athletics.* London, 1925.

177. ***Ziebarth, E.*** *Aus dem griechischen Schulwesen.* Leipzig-Berlin, 1909, (=1912).

178. ***Zsigmond, J.*** "A klasikus görög és jelenkori athlétika kozos jellemvonásai." ("The Common Characteristics of Classical Greek and Modern Athletics.") *Testnevelés* 1 (1928): 210-220.

179. ***Zsingor, M.*** "A régi kor hites athlétái." ("Famous Athletes of Antiquity.") *Tornaügy* 5 (1887-88): 34-38. (Depping W. nyomán közli-).

II

THE ORIGIN AND DEVELOPMENT OF GREEK ATHLETICS

A. Minoan and Mycenaean Athletics

180. ***Alvarez de Miranda, A.*** *Ritos y juegos del toro.* Madrid, 1962.
Review: AP 1964: *Zephyrus* 13 (1962): 125-126 Blázquez.

181. ***Biliński, B.*** "Antyczni krytycy antycznego sportu, I." *Meander* 11 (1956) fasc. 9: 286-308.

182. ***Bilinski, B.*** "Antyczni krytycy antycznego sportu, I." *Meander* 11 (1956) fasc. 10-11: 365-387.

183. ***Brumbaugh, R. S.*** "The Knossos Game-Board." *AJA* 2nd Series, 79 (April, 1975): 135-136.

184. ***Catling, H. W.*** "A Mycenaean Puzzle from Lefkandi in Euboea." *AJA* 2nd Series, 72 (January, 1968): 41-49. (chariot.)

185. ***Graham, J. W.*** "The Central Court as the Minoan Bull Ring." *AJA* 61 (1957): 255-262.

186. ***Harrison, Richard.*** "The 'Bull-Cult' in Ancient Crete." *History Today* 28 (1978): 28-35.

187. ***Howell, M. L.*** "Sealstones of the Minoan period in the Ashmolean Museum, Oxford." *Research Quarterly* 40 (1969): 509-517.

188. ***Howell, M. L.*** "Sport und Spiele im minoischen Kreta." *Geschichte der Leibesuebungen* H. Ueberhorst, ed., vol. 1: 229-259. See no. 162.

189. ***Lende, O.*** "Das kretische Stiersprungspiel." *Marburger Wincklemann-Programm.* 1965: 30-37.

190. ***Littauer, M. A.*** "The Military Use of the Chariot in the Aegean in the LBA." *AJA* 2nd Series, 76 (April, 1972): 145-157.

191. ***Lukas, G.*** *Die Koerperkultur in fruehen Epochen der Menschheitsentwicklung,* see no. 94.

192. ***Matz, F.,*** "The Zenith of Minoan Civilization," Ch. XII in *The Cambridge Ancient History* vol. II, pt. 1 (Cambridge, 1973).

193. ***Mylonas, G. E.*** "The Figured Mycenaean Stelai." *AJA* 2nd Series, 55, No. 2 (1955): 134-147. Depiction of chariot race.

194. ***Platon, N.*** "Sir Arthur Evans and the Creto-Mycenaean Bullfights." *Greek Heritage* 1, No. 4 (1964) 91-93.

195. ***Popplow, U.*** "Stierspiele in Altkreta." *Die Leibeserziehung* 13 (1964): 33-46.

196. ***Popplow, U.*** "Totenkult und Wagenrennen im Alt-Mykene." *Die Leibeserziehung* 8 (1958): 210-215, 248-252.

197. ***Reichel, A.*** "Die Stierspiel in der kretisch-mykenischen Kultur." *MDAI(A)* 34 (1909): 85-99.

198. ***Ridington, W. R.*** *The Minoan-Mycenaean Background of Greek Athletics.* Diss: Univ. of Pennsylvania, 1935.

199. ***Sakellarakis, J.*** "Athletics in Crete and Mycenae." *The Eternal Olympics,* N. Yalouris, ed. New York, 1976: 13-23.

200. ***Sliwa, J.*** "Zeglarstwo kreténskie." *Filomata* 178 (1964): 411-420.

201. ***Snethlage, H. C.*** "De geknevelde stier." *Hermeneus* 35 (1964): 280-282.

202. ***Ward, A.*** "The Cretan Bull Sports." *Antiquity* 42 (1968): 117-122.

203. ***Younger, J. G.*** "Bronze Age Representations of Aegean Bull-leaping." *AJA* 80 (1976): 125-137.

B. Athletics in Homer and in Greek Myth

204. ***Andronikos, M.*** "Totenkult." *Archaeologica Homerica 3W. Die Denkmaeler und das fruehgriechische Epos. Auftr. des Dt. Archaeol. Inst.* F. Matz and H. G. Buchholz, eds. Goettingen: Vandenhoeck & Ruprecht, 1968.

205. ***Brelich, A.*** *Guere, agoni e culti nella Grecia arcaica.* Antiquitas 1. Reihe: Abh. zur alten Gesch. 7. Bonn: Habelt, 1961.

Reviews: AP 1961: *AC* 30 (1961) 642-643 Berger. *REG* 74 (1961) 304-305 Will.

206. ***Buchholz, H. G.*** and ***Karageorghis, V.*** "Homeric aiganee." *AAA* 3 (1970): 386-391.

207. ***Decker, W.*** "Zur Bogenprobe des Odysseus." *KBSW* 6 (1977): 149ff.

208. ***Delebeque, E.*** *Le cheval dans l'Iliade, suivi d'un Lexique du cheval chez Homère et d'un Essai sur le cheval préhomérique.* Etudes & Comment 9. Paris: Klincksieck, 1951.

Reviews: AP 1951: *LEC* 19 (1951): 440 Delande. *MH* 8 (1951): 312 Redard. *RPh* 25 (1951): 289-291 Chantraine.

209. ***Ebert, J.*** "Zu mythischen Agonen und zum Problem des agonalen Wesens der Griechen." *Stadion* 2 (1976): 307-314. (Concerns I. Weiler. *Der Agon in Mythos.* (1974).) See no. 225.

210. ***Goehler, J.*** "Ein Sportfest bei den Phaiaken." *Gymnasium* 56 (1959): 196-200.

211. ***Howland, R. L.*** "Epeius, Carpenter and Athlete (or what made the Achaeans laugh at *Iliad* 23, 840.)" *PCPhS* 183 (1954-1955): 15-16.

212. ***Howland, R. L.*** "Nestor and the Chariot Race." *PCPhS* 181 (1950-1951): 30.

213. ***Leaf, W.*** "The Homeric Chariot." *JHS* 5 (1884): 185-194.

214. ***Lesky, A.*** "Peleus." *RE* 19, 1. Stuttgart, 1937: coll. 217-308.

215. ***Meuhll, P. von der.*** "Einige Gedanken zum *psi* der Ilias." *MH* 18 (1961): 198-203.

216. ***Meuli, K.*** "Der griechische Agon. Kampf und Kampfspiel im Totenbrauch, Totentanz, Totenklage und Totenlob." Basler Habilitationsschrift 1926, posthumously edited (with additions) by Histor. Seminar der Deutschen Sporthochschule. Cologne, 1968: 57ff.

217. ***Muth, R.*** "*Mens sana*...und Odysseus." *Sport und Universitaet.* F. Fetz, ed. Innsbruck, 1972: 13-20.

218. ***O'Neal, W. J.*** "Fair Play in Homeric Greece." *CB* 56 (1979): 11ff.

219. ***Patroni, G.*** "I ludi athletici presso i Faeci." *Miscellanea G. Galbiati.* Milan: Hoepli, 1951. vol. 1: 5ff.

220. ***Pleket, H. W.*** "Zur Soziologie des antiken Sports." *Mededelingen Nederlands Instituut te Rome* 36 (1974): 57-87.

221. ***Pope, A.*** *Die Gymnastik bei Homer und ihre grundlagende Bedeutung fuer die Gestaltung der spaeteren Gymnastik.* Diss.: Rostock, 1936.

222. ***Richardson, L. J. D.*** "Homeric *aiganee* again." *AAA* 4 (1971): 262-263.

223. ***Roller, L. E.*** *Funeral Games in Greek Literature, Art and Life.* Thesis: Univ. of Pennsylvania, 1977: 50-55.

224. ***Vries, G. J. de.*** "De prijsuitreking in Ilias 23." *Hermeneus* 31 (1960): 208-214.

225. ***Weiler, I.*** *Der Agon im Mythos. Zur Einstellung der Griechen zum Wettkampf.* Impulse der Forsch. 16. Darmstadt: Wiss. Buchges., 1974.

Reviews: AP 1980: *GB* 8 (1979): 277-281 Eisenberger. AP 1978: *Helmantica* 27 (1976): 541 Ruiz. *AAHG* 30 (1977): 194-197 Muth. AP 1976: *WS N. F.* 10 (1976): 264 Petersmann. *Stadion* 2 (1976): 307-314 Ebert.

226. ***Weiler, I.*** *Agonales in Wettkaempfen der griechischen Mythologie.* Veroeff. der Univ. Innsbruck 19. Innsbruck Univ., 1969.

Reviews: AP 1971: *CR* 21 (1971): 467 Harris. AP 1970: *Gymnasium* 77 (1970): 554-555 Schwarz.

227. ***Weiler, I.*** *"AIEN ARISTEUEIN.* Ideologiekritische Bemerkungen zu einem vielzitierten Homerwort." *Stadion* 1 (1975): 200-227.
228. ***Willcock, M. M.*** "The Funeral Games of Patroclus." *BICS* 20 (1973): 1-11.
229. ***Willimczik, K.*** *Leibesuebungen bei Homer.* Schorndorf bei Stuttgart: K. Hofmann, 1969.

C. Athletics in Archaic and Classical Greece

230. ***Boelte, F.*** "Platanistas." *RE* 20, 2. Stuttgart, 1950: coll. 2333-2334.
231. ***Borthwick, E.K.*** "The Gymnasium of Bromius." *JHS* 84 (1964): 49-53.
232. ***Breuckner, A.*** "Kerameikos-Studien. Der *epitáphos agón* im 5. Jh." *MDAI(A)* 35 (1910): 200-210.
233. ***Bussemaker.*** "Gymnastes." *D.-S.* 2, 2. Paris, 1896: 1698-1699.
234. ***Bussemaker*** and ***Fougères, G.*** "Gymnastica." *D.-S.* 2, 2. Paris, 1896: 1699-1705.
235. ***Christiansen, J.*** "Gyldne laegeraad saerlight om diaet. Copenhagen: Gyldendal, 1933.
Review: AP 1936: *Isis* 25 (1936): 520-521 Mead.
236. ***Crowther, N. B.*** "Weightlifting in Antiquity. Achievement and Training." *G&R* 24 (1977): 111-120.
237. ***Diem, C.*** "Sportdiaet, I: Antike." *Olympische Rdsch.* 11 (1940): 1-2.
238. ***Eckmann, G.*** *Ueber die praktische Rolle der Diaetetik in der hippokratischen Medizin.* Diss.: Berlin, 1936.
239. ***Edelstein, L.*** "Antike Diaetetik." *Ant* 1931: 255-270.
240. ***Eisen, G.*** "The Role of Women in Ancient Fertility Cults and the Origin of Sport." See no. 29.
241. ***Eisen, G.*** *Sports and Women in Antiquity.* See no. 28.
242. ***Fontenrose, J.*** "The Hero as Athlete." *CSCA* 1 (1968): 73-104.
243. ***Forbes, C. A.*** "Crime and Punishment in Greek Athletics." *CJ* 47 (1951/52): 169-173 and 202.
244. ***Fougères, G.*** *"Paidotribes."* *D.-S.* 4, 1. Paris, 1907: 277-278.
245. ***Girard, P.*** *"Kosmetes."* *D.-S.* 3, 2. Paris, 1904: 865.
246. ***Girard, P.*** *"Paidonomos."* *D.-S.* 4, 1. Paris, 1907: 276-277.
247. ***Girard, P.*** *"Sophronistes."* *D.-S.* 4, 2. Paris, s. a.: 1399-1400.

248. *Glotz, G.* "*Gymnasiarchia.*" *D.-S.* 2, 2. Paris, 1896: 1675-1684.
249. *Glotz, G.* "*Xystos.*" *D.-S.* 5. Paris, 1914: 1027-1031.
250. *Goeber, W.* "*Palaistra 2*" *RE* 18, 2. Stuttgart, 1942: Col. 2497.
251. *Goehler, J.* "Olympioniken als Krieger und Politiker: Zur sozialen Stellung der Olympia-Sieger im Altertum." *Die Leibeserziehung* 19 (1970): 190-195.
252. *Harris, H. A.* "El aficionado y el profesional en el deporte griego y romano." *CAF* 14, 1 (1972): 69-87.
253. *Juethner, J.* "*Gymnastes.*" *RE* 7, 2. Stuttgart, 1912:coll. 2026-2030.
254. *Juethner, J.* "*Gymnastik.*" *RE* 7, 2. Stuttgart, 1912: coll. 2030-2085.
255. *Juethner, J.* "*Kalokagathia.*" *Charisteria. Alois Rzach zum 80. Geburtstag dargebracht,* 1930: 99-119.
256. *Juethner, J.* "*Paidotribes.*" *RE* 18, 2. Stuttgart, 1942: coll. 2389-2396.
257. *Karouzou, S.* "Scènes de palestre." *BCH* 86 (1962): 430-466.
258. *Kornexl, E.* "Begriff und Einschaetzung der Gesundheit des Koerpers in der griechischen Literatur von ihren Anfaengen bis zum Hellenismus." *Commentationes Aenipotanae* 21. Innsbruck: Wagner, 1970.
259. *Lawińska-Tyszkowska, J.* "Le rôle de l'entraîneur dans la Grèce ancienne." (in Russian) *Acta Conventus* 11 *Eirene,* 21-25 oct. 1958. Warszaw Acad. Sceint., 1971: 55-61.
260. *Lennartz, K.* *Geschichte des Frauensports. Bibliographie. Geschichte der Leibesuebungen.* Sportbibliographische Veroeffentlichungen des Seminars fuer Leibeserziehung. Cologne, 1974.
261. *Luni, M.* "Documenti per la storia della istituzione ginnasiale e dell'attivita athletica in Cirenaica." *QAL* 8 (1976): 223-284.
262. *Mannings, C. A.* "Professionalism in Greek Athletics." See no. 97.
263. *Marcovich, M.* "Xenophanes on Drinking-parties and Olympic Games." *ICS* 3 (1978): 1-26.
264. *Matz, D.* "The Development of Professionalism in Greek Athletics." *NASSH Proceedings* 1978: 4f.
265. *Meinburg, E.* "Gymnastische Erziehung in der Platonischen Paideia." *Arena(=Stadion)* 1 (1975): 228-266.

266. ***Miller, J.*** "Melesias 1." *RE* 15, 1. Stuttgart, 1931: col. 495.

267. ***Modrze, A.*** "Milon 2." *RE* 15, 2. Stuttgart, 1932: coll. 1672-1676.

268. ***Musiolek, P.*** "Die Anschauungen des Aristoteles ueber koerperliche Erziehung als Teil der Paideia in ihrem historischen Zusammenhang." *StudClas* 4 (1962): 95-124.

269. ***Muth, R.*** "Der Sieg in Olympia: Faszination und Kritik." *Wort im Gebirge* 25 (1976): 7-39.

270. ***Mylonas, G. E.*** "Athletic Honors in the Fifth Century." *CJ* 39 (1943-1944): 278-289.

271. ***Oehler, J.*** *"Gymnasíarkhos."* *RE* 7, 2. Stuttgart, 1912: coll. 1969-2004.

272. ***Oehler, J.*** *"Gymnasium."* *RE* 7, 2. Stuttgart, 1912: coll. 2004-2026.

273. ***Oehler, J.*** *"Sophronistaí."* *RE* 3 A, 1. Stuttgart, 1927: coll. 1104-1106.

274. ***Patrucco, R.*** "L'attivita sportiva di Sparta." *Archaeologica. Scritti in onore di Aldo Neppi-Modona, a cura di Caffarello, N.* Florence: Olschki, 1975: 395-412.

275. ***Philipp, H.*** "Kroton 1." *RE* 11, 2. Stuttgart, 1922: coll. 2020-2026.

276. ***Pleket, H. W.*** "Games, Prizes and Ideology. Some Aspects of the History of Sport in the Greco-Roman World." *Stadion* 1 (1975): 49-89.

277. ***Pleket, H. W.*** "Some Aspects of the Athletic Guilds." *ZPE* 10 (1973): 197-227.

278. ***Preisigke, F.*** *"Kosmetés."* *RE* 11, 2. Stuttgart, 1922: coll. 1490-1495.

279. ***Reisch, E.*** *"Aleiptes."* *RE* 1, 1. Stuttgart, 1893: coll. 1360-1362.

280. ***Reisch, E.*** *"Anagkophagía."* *RE* 1, 2. Stuttgart, 1894: coll. 2058-2060.

281. ***Rudolph, W.*** "Sportverletzungen und Sportschaeden in der Antike." *Altertum* 22 (1976): 21-26.

282. ***Rudolph, W.*** "Zu den Formen des Berufssports zur Zeit der Poliskrise." *Hellenische Poleis.* Welskopf, E. Ch., ed. Berlin: Akad.-Verl., 1974: 1472-1483.

283. ***Schneider, K.*** *"Palaístra* 1." *RE* 18, 2. Stuttgart, 1942: coll. 2472-2497.

284. ***Schulthess, O.*** *"Paidonómoi."* *RE* 18, 2. Stuttgart, 1942: coll. 2387-2389.

285. ***Saundeau, R.*** and ***Saundeau-Deterne, C.*** *La renaissance de la gymnastique médicale. Mercurialis (chapitre sur la gymnastique dans l'antiquité).* Clermond-Ferrand Librarie Queyriaux, 1943.

Review: AP 1952: *RHS* 1 (1947): 272-273 Brunet.

286. ***Wade-Gery, H. T.*** "Militiades." *JHS* 71 (1951): 212-221.

287. ***Weirich, R.*** *Koerper und Koerpererziehung bei Platon.* Diss: Munich, Endigen Wild, 1932.
Review: AP 1933: *PhW* 1933: 993 Paulu.

287a. ***Young, D. C.***, "Professionalism and Amateurism in Archaic and Classical Greek Athletics", *AnW* 7 (1983) 45-51.

287b. ***Young, D. C.***, *The Myth of Greek Amateur Athletics,* Chicago: Ares, 1984.

288. ***Ziehen, L.*** "Sparta (E. Spartanische Kulte)." *RE* A, 2. Stuttgart, 1929: col. 1453-1525.

289. ***Zucker, F.*** *"Gymnasíarkhos kómes." Aegyptus* 11 (1930-1931): 485-496.

D. Hellenistic Greek Athletics and the Ephebia

290. ***Brown, T. S.*** "Alexander and Greek Athletics, in Fact and Fiction." *Greece and the Eastern Mediterranean in Ancient History and Prehistory. Studies Presented to Fritz Schachermeyer on the Occasion of His 80 Birthday.* Kinze, K. H., ed. Berlin: de Gruyter, 1977: 76-88.

291. ***Diem, C.*** *Alexander der Grosse als Sportmann.* Frankfurt a. M., 1957.

292. ***Dow, S.*** "The Athenian Epheboi." *TAPA* 91 (1960): 381-409.

293. ***Dow, S.*** "The Athenian Honors for Aristonikos of Karystos, Alexander's *sphairistes." HSCP* 67 (1963): 77-92.

294. ***Dumont, A.*** *Essai sur l'éphébie attique.* 2 vols. Paris, 1968. (repr. of 1875-1876 edition.)

295. ***Forbes, C. A.*** "Ancient Athletic Guilds." *CPh* 50 (1955): 238-252.

296. ***Gerassimov, Th.*** "Corona donatica sur une liste d'éphébes d'Odessos. (in Bulgarian) *BIAB* 13 (1939): 332-335.

297. ***Girard, P.*** *"Ephebi." D.-S.* 2. 1. Paris, 1892: 621-636.

298. ***Krischen, F.*** "Das hellenistische Gymnasion von Priene." *JDAI* 38/39 (1923-1924): 133-150.

299. ***Moretti, L.*** *"KOINA ASIAS." RFIC* N.S. 32 (1954): 276-289.

300. ***Nilsson, M. P.*** *Die hellenistische Schule.* Munich: Beck, 1955.

301. ***Oehler, J.*** *"Ephébarkhos." RE* 5, 2. Stuttgart, 1905: coll. 2735-2736.

302. ***Oehler, J.*** *"Ephébía." RE* 5, 2. Stuttgart, 1905: coll. 2737-2746.

303. ***Pelekidis, Chrysis.*** *Histoire de l'éphébie attique des origines à 31 avant Jésus-Christ.* Paris, 1962.

304. ***Picard, Ch.*** "Les fouilles allemandes au stade d'Olympie et l'histoire des jeux sacrés." *RA* 1 (1961): 217-221.

305. ***Pleket, H. W.*** "*Collegium juvenum Nemesiarum.* A Note on Ancient Youth-organizations (activités sportives.)" *Mnemosyne* 22 (1969): 281-298.

306. ***Pleket, H. W.*** "Sport und Leibesuebungen in der griechischen Welt des hellenistisch-roemischen Zeitalters." *Geschichte der Leibesuebungen* vol 2: 280-311. See Ueberhorst, no. 162.

307. ***Reinmuth, O. W. R.*** "*Ephebia.*" *KP* 2. Stuttgart: Druckenmueller, 1967: 287-291.

308. ***Reinmuth, O. W. R.*** *The Ephebic Inscriptions of the Fourth Century B.C. Mnemosyne Suppl.* 14: Leiden Brill, 1971.

Reviews: AP 1971: *AC* 41 (1972): 714-715 Roesch. *RFIC* 100 (1972): 509-511 Virgilio.

309. ***Reinmuth, O. W. R.*** "The Genesis of the Athenian Ephebia." *TAPA* 83 (1952): 34-50.

310. ***Reynolds, J.*** and ***Mason, O.*** "Une inscription éphébique de Ptolemais (Cyrenaique)." *ZPE* 20 (1976): 87-100.

311. ***Rigsby, K. J.*** "Sacred Ephebic Games at Oxyrhynchus." *CE* 52 (1977) No. 103: 147-155.

312. ***Ruschenbusch, E.*** "Die soziale Herkunft der Epheben um 330." *ZPE* 35 (1973): 173-176.

313. ***Wilhelm, H. E.*** "Taegliche Gesundheitspflege im 4. Jh v. Chr." *LKE* 54 (1933): 144-146.

III

THE ANCIENT OLYMPICS

A. General and Miscellaneous

314. ***Angeli Bernardini, P.*** "Ancora sull'iscrizione agonistische di Kleomrotos." *QUCC* 26 (1977): 149-154.
315. ***Angeli Bernardini, P.*** "I giochi olimpici nell'antichità." *QUCC* 16 (1973): 155-161.
316. ***Assa, J.*** "El Olimpismo feminino." *CAF* 2 (1960): 397ff.
317. ***Beloch, J.*** "Die Siegerliste von Olympia." *Hermes* 64 (1929): 192-199.
318. ***Bengtson, H.*** *Die olympischen Spiele in der Antike.* Lebendige: Antike Zuerich Artemis-Verl., 1971.
    Reviews: AP 1975: *Eirene* 13 (1975): 152-153 Olivová. AP 1972: *DLZ* 92 (1971): 1038-1040 Wirth. *REL* 49 (1971): 480 Jean Durry.
319. ***Bickel, A.*** *Die Ernaehrung der olympischen Kaempfer in Vergangenheit und Gegenwart.* Berlin, 1938. (Buecher d. Hygiene u. Volksernaehrung 3.)
320. ***Bland, E. A.*** *Olympic Story.* London, 1948.
321. ***Boetticher, A.*** *Olympia. Das Feste und seine Staette.* Berlin, 1886.[2]
322. ***Buhmann, H.*** *Der Sieg in Olympia und in den anderen panhellenischen Spielen.* Diss: Munich: 1972 Munich Verl. UNI-Druck, 1972.
323. ***Catuadella, M. R.*** "La prostasia sugli agoni olimpici nella Ol. 8ª." *RAL* 19 (1964): 66-74.
324. ***Corsini,*** Ed. *Dissertationes 4. agonisticae quibus Olympiorum, Pythiorum, Nemeorum atque Isthmiorum tempus inquiritur ac demonstratur. Accedit hieronicarum catalogus editis longe uberior et accuratior.* Leipzig, 1752.
325. ***Curtius, E.*** "Entwurf einer Geschichte von Olympia." *Olympia. Die Ergebnisse der von dem Deutschen Reich veranstelteten Ausgrabungen.* vol. I. Berlin, 1897.
326. ***Curtius, E.*** *Olympia. Mit ausgewaehlten Texten von Pindar, Pausanias, Lukian.* Anh.: J. Ascherfeld: Die olympischen Kampfarten und die Leibesuebungen der Griechen im Spiegel ihres Schrifttums (161-184). Berlin: Atlantis, 1935.
327. ***Curtius, E.*** "Olympia. Ein Vortrag." *Ant* 12 (1936): 229-252.
328. ***Diels, H.*** "Die Olympionikenliste aus Oxyrhinckos." *Hermes* 36 (1901): 72ff.

329. ***Diem, C.*** *Ewiges Olympia.* Bad Oeynhausen/Berlin/ Frankfurt a. M./Leipzig, 1948.

330. ***Diem, C.*** *776 v. Chr. - Olympiaden - 1964. Eine Geschichte des Sports.* Stuttgart, 1964.

331. ***Doell, H.*** "Ideal und Idol in Olympia." *Die Leibesuebungen* 1960: 152-157.

332. ***Drees, L.*** *Olympia: Gods, Artists. and Athletes.* Gerald Ohn, Engl. trans. N. Y. and Wash.: Praeger, 1968. Original German edition: Stuttgart: Kohlhammer, 1967.

333. ***Ebert, J.*** *et al.* eds. *Olympia von den Anfaengen bis zu Coubertin.* Leipzig: Koehler and Amelang, 1980. Also under the title *Olympia. Mythos und Geschichte moderne Wettkaempfe.* Wien: Tusch, 1980.

334. ***Ebert, J.*** "Olympia-Olympische Spiele. Zu einigen Aspekten des Sports und des Athletenbildes der Antike." *Altertum* 22 (1976): 5-20.

335. ***Ferguson, J.*** "Olympia and Ancient Athletics." *N&C* 8 (1965): 1-9.

336. ***Feretti, L.*** *Olimpiadi.* Milan, 1959.[2]

337. ***Finley, M. I.*** and ***Pleket, H. W.*** *The Olympic Games. The First Thousand Years.* New York: Viking, 1976.
German translation: *Die Olympischen Spiele in der Antike.* Tuebingen: Wunderliche, 1976.

Reviews: AP 1978: *CW* 71 (1978): 406-407 Sweet. AP 1977: *G&R* 24 (1977): 97 Walcot. *JHS* 97 (1977): 199-200 Howland. AP 1976: *NYRB* 23, 19 (1976): 23-24 Brown. *Hermathena* 120 (1976): 76-80 Wilson.

338. ***Foerster, G. H.*** "Die Sieger in den olympischen Spielen bis zur Ende des 4. Jh. v. Chr." (2 part article). *Bericht ueber das Schuljahr, Gymnasium zu Zwickau.* 1891: 1-30. 1892: 1-32. (1922).[2]

339. ***Fugardi, A.*** *Storia delle Olimpiadi: Collana universale 19.* Bologna: Cappelli, 1958.

340. ***Furber, P.*** "The Olympic Games." *Pegasus* 1 (juin 1964): 27-29.

341. ***Gardiner, E. N.*** "The Alleged Kingship of the Olympic Victor." *ABSA* 22 (1916-1917, 1917-1918): 85-106.

342. ***Gardiner, E. N.*** *Olympia. Its History and Remains.* Oxford, 1925.

343. ***Gasper, C.*** "Olympia." *D.-S.* 4, 1., Paris, 1907: 172-196.

344. ***Gerstenberg, J.*** *Die Wiedergewinnung Olympias als Staette und Idee.* Diss.: Tuebingen, 1947.

345. ***Gilbert, G.*** *De anagraphis Olympiis commentatio.* Progr. Gotha, 1875.

346. ***Gross, W. H.*** "Quos iconicas vocant. Zur Portraetcharakter der Statuen dreimaliger olympischer Sieger." *NAWG* 1969: 3.

347. *Hachtmann, K. Olympia und seine Festspiele.* Guetersloh, 1899.

348. **Hampl, F.** "Die Olympischen Spiele in Altertum." *Olympia einst und jetzt. Vortragsreihe der Universitaet Innsbruck und des Kulturamtes der Stadt Innsbruck aus Anlass der 9. Olympischen Winterspiele 1964.* Schriftleit. Muth, R., Zusammenstell. des Bildteiles Wotschitzky, A.: Innsbruck Selbstverl. des Stadtmagistrates, 1964: 9-20.

349. *Harbott, R. Olympia und die olympischen Spiele von 776 v. Chr. bis heute.* Berlin: Limpert, 1935.[2]

350. *Harder, R.* "Das alte Griechenland: die Heimat der olympischen Spiele." *LKE* 55 (1936): 343-350.

351. *Harder, R. Wettkaempfe im Zeichen der olympischen Ringen von der Antike bis Squaw-Valley und Rom.* Hannover, 1960.

352. *Hege, W.* and ***Rodenwaldt, G.*** *Olympia.* Berlin, 1936.

353. *Herendi, A. Milyen volt az okor ólimpiásza? (What Were the Olympic Games Like?)* Budapest, 1925.

354. *Herrmann, H. V.* "Olympia und seine Spiele im Wandel der Zeiten. Mit 7 Plaenen." *Gymnasium* 80 (1973): 172-205.

355. *Hilker, F. Die olympischen Spiele im Altertum und Gegenwart.* Leipzig, 1936.

356. *Hjortsoe, L., Olympia. Den Graeske Olympiade.* Copenhagen: Gylendale, 1960.

357. *Hoenle, A. Olympia in der Politik der Griechischen Staatenwelt.* Diss.: Tuebingen, 1968. (=Bebenhausen, 1972).

358. *Hugill, W. M.* "Olympics Old and New." *Phoenix* 11, No. 1 (Spring, 1949): 31-39.

359. *Hyde, W. W. De olympionicarum statuis a Pausania commemoratis.* Diss.: Halle, 1903.

360. *Janell, W.* "Chronicon Olympicum." *Klio* 21 (1927): 344-349.

361. *Jantzen, U., **Thiemann, E.*** and ***Mallwitz, A.,*** *Olympia in der Antike. Ausstellung in Essen 18 Juni bis 28 August, 1960.* Katalog. Essen, 1960.

362. *Juethner, J.* "Das Alter der olympischer Spiele." *Geistige Arbeit.:* Berlin, 1937: 3-6.

363. *Juethner, J.* "*Eiselastikós agón* (certamen iselasticum)." *RE* 5, 2. Stuttgart, 1905: col. 2141.

364. *Kaldis-Henderson, N. A Study of Women in Ancient Elis.* Unpublished diss.: U. Minn., 1979. *DA* 40 (1979): 3456A.

365. *Kárpáti, K.* "Olympia múltja és jelene." ("The Past and Present Olympia.") *Görög földön. Emlékkönyv a magyar tanárok 1893-ik évi tanulmányútjáról.* Budapest, 1895: 35-56.

366. ***Kempe, H.*** "Hatten Jungfrauen Zutritt zu den olympischen Spielen?" *LKE* 55 (1936): 281-282.

367. ***Kerestényi, J.*** *Az olympiák története. Olympiától Mexikóig. (The History of the Olympic Games: From Olympia to Mexico.)* Budapest, 1968. (2 ed. *Olympiától Muenchenig.* Budapest, 1972. 3 ed. Olympiától Montréalig. Budapest, 1976.)

368. ***Kerestényi, J.*** "Jeux Olympiques à Daphne (in Hungarian)" *Antik tanulmányok* 8 (1961): 221-242. cf. summary in *BCO* 8 (1963): 197-198.

369. ***Kieran, J.*** and ***Daely, A.*** *The Story of the Olympic Games 776 B.C. - 1956 A.D.* Philadelphia and New York, 1957.

370. ***Klincsek, J.*** "Az olympiai játékokról." ("About the Olympic Games.") *Tornaügy* 5 (1887-88): 42-44.

371. ***Klincsek, J.*** "Az olympusi versenyeken usuban volt törvények." ("The Olympic Competitions Used Rules.") *A "sport-Világ Albuma".* 1895-96: 4-7. (= *Tornaügy* 4 (1886-87): 46-47.)

372. ***Klincsek, J.*** "Morális jutalmazás az olympusi versenyeken." ("Moral Rewards in the Olympic Games.") *Tornaügy* 4 (1886-87): 54-55.

373. ***Koerte, A.*** "Die Enstehung der Olympionikenlisten." *Hermes* 39 (1904): 224-243.

374. ***Kolobova, K. M.*** and ***Oscherka, E. L.*** *Olympische Spiele.* Moscow, 1958. (in Russian).

375. ***Krause, J. H.*** *Olympia, oder Darstellung der grossen olympischen Spiele und der damit verbundenen Festlichkeiten.* Vienna, 1938. Vol. 3 of idem, *Hellenicá,* 4 vols, Leipzig, 1841.

376. ***Kreutz, F.*** *Der wahre olympische Geist und das Griechentum* Heidelberg, 1936.

377. ***Laemmer, M.*** "Der Diskos des Asklepiades aus Olympia und das Marmor Parium." *ZPE* 1 (1967): 107-109.

378. ***Laemmer, M.*** "The Nature and Function of the Olympic Truce in Ancient Greece." *History of Physical Education and Sport* 3 (1975/76): 37-52.

379. ***Lambros, S. P.*** and ***Politis, N. G.*** *Die Olympischen Spiele 776-1896.* Athens/Leipzig, 1896.

380. ***Lang, N.*** "Olympia." ("Olympia") *Ókori Lexikon 2.* Pecz, V. ed. Budapest, 1904: 253-268.

381. ***Langlotz, E.*** "Die Bedeutung der neuen Funde in Olympia." *Das Neue Bild der Antike.* Vol. 1. Leipzig, 1942: 155-171.

382. ***Lennartz, K.*** *Kenntnisse und Vorstellungen von Olympia und den Olympischen Spielen in der Zeit von 393-1896. Theorie der Leibeserziehung.* 9. Schorndorf: Hofmann, 1974.

383. ***Lévêque, P.*** "Des dieux et des jeux d'Olympie." *REG* 87 (1974): 341-344.

384. ***Lukas, G.*** "Olympische Spiele - Olympische Idee." *Theoria und Praxis der Koerperkultur.* 1.Jhg. H. 4 (1952): 29-40.

385. ***Maisto, A.*** *Gli Italici nei ginochi panellenici.* 1923.

386. ***Malteso, G. Th.*** *Olympia.* Kaiserslautern, 1959.

387. ***Marcucci, C.*** and ***Scaringi, C.*** *Olimpiadi, storia delle Olimpiadi antiche e moderne.* Milan, 1959.

388. ***Marly, C.*** "Les Jeux olympiques." *Sciences & Avenir* (août 1960): 410-416.

389. ***Maróti, E.*** "Currus Achaicus." *AT* 13 (1966): 70-76. (in Hungarian) = *AAntHung* 14 (1966): 359-369. (in German).

390. ***Mehl, E.*** " "Olympia" der "Olympiade"." *Festgabe Mehl*-Anhang: 117-119. (=*Muttersprache,* Lueneburg, 1956). See Jahn, *Zur Weltgeschichte de Leibesuebungen,* no. 62.

391. ***Melber, H.*** and ***Steeger, Th.*** *Olympia und die Olympischen Spiele.* Bamberg, 1936.

392. ***Melber, J.*** *Olympia. Aufstieg und Verfall der Olympischen Spiele, ihr Untergang und ihre Wiederbelebung in der Gegenwart.* Munich and Berlin, 1936.

393. ***Merkelbach, R.*** *"Olympeíeia."* *ZPE* 12 (1973): 210.

394. ***Mezö, F.*** "Az olympiai játékok története." ("The History of the Olympic Games.") *Testnevelés* 1 (1928): 379-400, 517-544, 635-653, 827-835.

395. ***Mezö, F.*** *Az olympiai játékok törénte. (The History of the Olympic Games.)* Budapest, 1929, 1978.[2]

396. ***Mezö, F.*** "Egy kis nyelvészkedés - a sportban. Az olympiai játékok helyes elnevezése." ("A Little Philology in Sport: The Correct Term for the Olympic Games.") *Testneveles-Sport* 1 (1926): 48-49.

397. ***Mezö, F.*** *Geschichte der olympischen Spiele.* Munich, 1930.

398. ***Mezö, F.*** "Der olympische Gedanke." *Das Altertum* 2 (1956): 161-169.

399. ***Mie, Fr.*** *Quaestiones agonisticae imprimis ad Olympiam pertinentes.* Diss.: Univ. Rostock. Rostock, 1888.

400. ***Molnár, S.*** "Az olympiai játékok." ("The Olympic Games.") *Hasznos Mulatságok* 2 (1936): 180ff.

401. ***Mommsen, A.*** *Ueber die Zeit der Olympien.* Leipzig, 1891.

402. ***Moretti, L.*** *Olympionikai. I vincitori negli antichi agoni Olimpici.* Rome, 1957.

403. ***Moretti, L.*** "Supplemento al Catalogo degli Olympionikai." *Klio* 52 (1970): 295-303.

404. ***Morgan, C. H.*** "Pheidias and Olympia." *Hesperia* 21, No. 4 (1952): 295-339.

405. ***Mousset, A.*** *Olympie et les jeux grecs:* Col. Les hauts lieux de l'histoire 14. Paris: Guillot, 1960.

Reviews: AP 1961: *LEC* 29 (1961): 227 Duval. *RBPh* 39 (1961): 1342 Delvoye. *Helmantica* 12 (1961): 417 Panyagua.

406. ***Mueller, O.*** "Die Phylen von Elis und Pisa." *RhM*[2] (1834): 176ff.

407. ***Muth, R.*** "Olympia: Faszination und Kritik." *Wort im Gebirge* 15 (1976): 7-39.

408. ***Muth, R.*** "Olympia, Idee und Wirklichkeit." *Serta Philologica Aenipontana* 3. Muth, R and Pfohl, G., eds. Innsbruck Beitr. zur Kulturwiss. 20 Innsbruck Verl. des Inst. fuer vergleich. Sprachwiss., 1979: 161-202.

409. ***Norberg, D.*** "L'olympionique, le poète et leur renom éternel." *Uppsala Univ. Arskrift,* 1945: 6.

410. ***Palaeologos, C.*** "The Reasons of Decline of the Ancient Olympic Games." *International Olympic Committee* (1971): 54-69.

411. ***Parandowski, J.*** *Les athlètes olympiques.* Translation from Polish by Cazin, P. Warsaw: Sport i Turystyka, 1960.

412. ***Pásztor, Á.*** "Olympiai játékok az ó-korban." ("The Olympic Games in Antiquity.") *Herkules* 13 (1896): 58-59.

413. ***Pere, A.*** *Les Jeux olympiques antiques.* pref. by Delorme, J. Bibl. de travail No. 413 Cannes Inst. coop. de l'Ecole mod., 1958.

414. ***Picard, Ch.*** "Les fouilles allemandes au stade d'Olympie et l'histoire des jeux sacrés." *RA* 1 (1961): 217-221.

415. ***Pleket, H. W.*** "Olympic Benefactors." *ZPE* 20 (1976): 1-18.

416. ***Poetscher, W.*** "Olympia. 2. Kulte." *KP* 4 (1972): 284-286.

417. ***Poole, L. & G.*** *The History of the Ancient Olympic Games.* London: Vision Press, 1965.

Review: AP 1967: *G&R* 14 (1967): 102 Sewter.

418. ***Poole, L. & G.*** "The Olympic Games of Greece." *Greek Heritage* 1, No. 4 (1964).

419. ***Popp, H.*** *Olympia. Ein Vermaechtnis der Griechen an die Nachwelt.* Berlin, 1935.

420. ***Popp, H.*** "Vom Sinn der olympischen Spiele." *Werk* (Duesseldorf) 15 (1935): 67-69.

421. ***Robert, C.*** "Die Ordnung der Olympischen Spiele und die Sieger der 75-83 Olympiade." *Hermes* 35 (1900): 141-195.

422. ***Robertson, N.*** "The Ancient Olympics. Sport, Spectacle and Ritual." *EMC* 20 (1976): 73-85.

423. ***Rudolph, W.*** *Olympische Spiele in der Antike.* Akzent 18. Leipzig: Urania-Verl., 1975.

424. ***Rudolph, W.*** *Olympischer Kampfsport in der Antike. Faustkampf, Ringkampf, und Pankration in der griechischen Nationalfestspielen.* Schr. der Sekt. fuer Altertumswiss. 47. Inst. fuer griech.-roem. Alterumsk. Berlin: Akad-Verl., 1965.

Reviews: AP 1967: *JHS* 87 (1967): 190-191 Harris. *CR* 17 (1967): 379-381 Harris. *DLZ* 88 (1967): 40-42 Ebert. AP 1966: *CW* 59 (1966): 261 Downey. *Gnomon* 38 (1966): 416-417 Reinmuth. *LF* 89 (1966): 197-198 Marek. *Erasmus* 18 (1966): 378-380 Bloch.

425. ***Rutgers, J.*** *Sextus Julius Africanus: Olympiadón anagraphé, adiectis ceteris, quae ex Olympionicarum fastis supersunt. Recensuit, commentario critico et indice Olympionicarum, instruxit -.* Leiden. Diss.: Univ. Leiden, 1862. Reprint, Chicago: Ares, 1980.

426. ***Sanin, Ju. V.*** *Les Jeux Olympiques et la poésie des Hellènes. Homère et les auteures lyriques classiques des 8e-5e ss. av. n. é.* (in Russian) Kiev Univ., 1980.

427. ***Scherer, Ch.*** *De Olympionicarum statuis.* Goettingen, 1885.

428. ***Schoebel, H.*** *The Ancient Olympic Games.* London: Studio Vista, 1966, and Princeton: van Nostrand, 1966.

Reviews: AP 1967: *Phoenix* 21 (1967): 152 McLeod. *G&R* 14 (1967): 102 Sewter. AP 1968: *CW* 61 (1968): 300 Downey.

429. ***Schoebel, H.*** *Olympia und seine Spiele.* Berlin: Akad.-Verl., 1965.

430. ***Schoebel, H.*** *Olympie et ses jeux.* Leipzig: Verl. fuer Kunst & Wiss., 1966.

Review: AP 1967: *LEC* 35 (1967): 102-103 Dumoulin.

431. ***Strempel, R.*** "Von der Urgeschichte der olympischen Spiele und vom olympischen Eid." *LKE* 12 (1936): 249.

432. ***Swaddling, J.*** *The Ancient Olympics.* London: Museum Publications, 1980.

433. ***Szanto.*** *"Ekekheiría." RE* 5, 2. Stuttgart, 1905: coll. 2162-2163.

434. ***Takács, M.*** "Az olympiai versenyek az ó-korban." ("Olympic Contests in Antiquity.") *Herkules* 12 (1895): 48-49.

435. ***Thiemann, E.*** "Die Olympischen Spiele im Altertum." *Olympia in der Antike. Ausstellung in Essen 18. Juni bis 28. August 1960.* Jantzen, U.; Thiemann, E.; and Mallwitz, E. & A., eds. Katalog: Essen, 1960.

436. ***Thorpe, J.*** and ***Collison, Th. F.*** *History of the Olympics.* Los Angeles: Wetzel, 1932.

437. ***Tostivint, R.*** "Les jeux olympiques dans l'antiquité." *BAGB* (1960): 445-458.

438. ***Ullrich, K.,*** *Olympische Spiele.* Berlin, 1978.

439. ***van der Veer, J. A. G.*** "De Olympisce spelen." *Hermeneus* 31 (1960): 190-196.

440. ***Weniger, L.*** "Der heilige Oelbaum in Olympia." *Jahresbericht ueber das Wilhelm-Ernstische Gymnasium in Weimar,* 1895.

441. ***Weniger, L.*** "Das Hochfest des Zeus in Olympia 1. Die Ordnung der Agone." *Klio* 4 (1904): 125-151.

442. ***Weniger, L.*** "Das Hochfest des Zeus in Olympia 2. Olympische Zeitenordnung." *Klio* 5 (1905): 1-38.

443. ***Weniger, L.*** "Das Hochfest des Zeus in Olympia 3. Der Gottesfriede." *Klio* 5 (1905): 184-194.

444. ***Weniger, L.*** "Die monatliche Opferung in Olympia." *Klio* 9 (1909): 291-303.

445. ***Yalouris, N.,*** ed. *The Eternal Olympics. The Art and History of Sports.* New Rochelle, N. Y.: Caratzas Brothers, 1979.

Review: *JSH* 7 (1980): 78-80 Forbes.

446. ***Yalouris, N.*** *The Olympic Games through the Ages.* New York, 1976. Contains survey of ancient games in *The Eternal Olympics* above, and review of modern Olympics movement.

447. ***Zeidler, H.*** "Olympia. Ein Beitrag zum Sprachgebrauch dieses Wortes." *Die Leibesuebungen* 8 (1932): 299-301.

448. ***Zelin, K. K.*** "Olimpioniki i tirany." *VDI* 82 (1962: 4): 21-29.

449. ***Ziehen, L.*** "Olympia (Olympische Spiele)." *RE* 17, 2. Stuttgart, 1937: coll. 2520-2536 and 18, 1. Stuttgart, 1939: coll. 1-71.

B. Origins

450. ***Bloch, R.*** "The Origins of the Olympic Games." *Scientific American* 219, Nr. 2 (1968): 78-85.

451. ***Boutros, L.*** *Phoenician Sport: Its Influence on the Origin of the Olympic Games.* Amsterdam: Gieben, 1981.

452. ***Cornford, F. M.*** "The Origin of the Olympic Games." in: J. E. Harrison, ed. *Themis.* Cambridge: The University Press, 1912: 212-259, reprinted N. Y.: University Books, 1962.

453. ***Drees, L.*** *Der Ursprung der Olympischen Spiele.* Beitr. zur Lehre & Forsch. der Leibeserziehung 13. Stuttgart-Schorndorf: Hofmann, 1962.

Reviews: AP 1967: *Humanitas* 15-16 (1963-1964): 549-551 da Rocha Pereira. AP 1966: *RFIC* 94 (1966): 347-350 Settis. *REA* 68 (1966): 161 Defradas. AP 1965: *Mnemosyne* 18 (1965): 438-439 van der Veer. *RPh* 39 (1965): 287-289 Vian. *AAHG* 17 (1964): 221 Hampl. AP 1964: *JHS* 84 (1964): 198-199 Pollard. *Gnomon* 36 (1964): 199 Pembroke. *Phoenix* 18 (1964): 85-87 McLeod. *AJA* 68 (1964): 314 Arnold. *CR* 14 (1964): 225 Boardman. *CJ* 59 (1964): 183 Forbes. *Emerita* 32 (1964): 355-357 Alsina. *AC* 33 (1964): 252-255 Servais. *RBPh* 42 (1964): 698 Donnay. *HZ* 199 (1964): 724 Gundel.

454. ***Goessler, P.*** "Das Pelops-Grab in Olympia und seine kultische Bedeutung." *Die Welt als Geschichte* 6 (1940): 283-292.

455. ***Kretschmer, P.*** "Die phrygische Episode in der Geschichte von Hellas." See no. 81.

456. ***Mahaffey, J. P.*** "On the Authenticity of the Olympic Register." *JHS* 2 (1881): 164-178.

457. ***Malten, L.*** "Leichenspiel und Totenkult." *MDAI (R)* 38/39 (1923-1924): 300-340.

458. ***Mathys, F. K.*** "Ursprung der Olympischen Spiele." *Sportmedizin* 3 (1953): 36-37.

459. ***Mehl, E.*** "Mutterrechtliche Reste in der Olympischen Festordnung." *Festschrift Carl Diem.* Koerbs, W.; Mies, H. and Wildt, K. C., eds. Frankfurt/M., Vienna: Limpert, 1962.

460. ***Meuli, K.*** "Der Ursprung der Olympischen Spiele." *Die Antike* 17 (1941): 189-208.

461. ***Miller, S. G.*** "The Date of Olympic Festivals." *MDAI(A)* 90 (1975): 215-231.

462. ***Montgomerey, H. C.*** "The Controversy about the Origins of the Olympic Games." *CW* 29 (1936): 169-174.

463. ***Nemirovsky, A. L.*** "L'origines des Jeux Olympiques." (in Russian) *VopIst* 6 (1980): 179-182.

464. ***Rose, H. G.*** "Greek Agones." See no. 143.

465. ***Ulf, Ch.*** and ***Weiler, I.*** "Der Ursprung der antiken Olympischen Spiele in der Forschung." *Stadion* 6 (1981): 1-38.

466. ***Vallois, R.*** "Les origines des jeux olympiques. Mythes et Réalités I. La course des Dactyles et Déméter Chamyné." *REA* 28 (1926): 305-322.

467. ***Vallois, R.*** "Les origines des jeux olympiques. Mythes et Réalités II. Pelops l'olympique." *REA* 31 (1929): 113-133.

468. ***Weniger, L.*** "Vom Ursprung der Olympischen Spiele." *RhM.* N. F. 72 (1917/18): 1-13.

C. The Site

469. ***Bernhart, M.*** "Die Olympischen Spiele auf antiken Muenzen." *Blaetter fuer Muenzfreunde* 71 (1936): 393ff.

470. ***Curtius, E.*** and ***Adler, F.*** *Olympia. Die Ergebnisse der von Deutschen Reich veranstalteten Ausgrabungen 1887-1897.* vols. 1-5. Berlin, 1890-1897.

471. ***Deubner, L.*** *Kult und Spiel im alten Olympia.* Leipzig: Keller, 1936.
Review: AP 1936: *GArb* 1936, 23: 13.

472. ***Dittenberger, W.*** and ***Purgold, K.*** *Die Inschriften von Olympia.* Berlin, 1942.

473. ***Doerpfeld, W.*** *Alt-Olympia. Untersuchungen und Ausgrabungen.* 2 vols. Berlin, 1935.

474. ***Drees, L.*** *Olympia: Gods, Artists and Athletes.* See no. 332.

475. ***Dyer, Louis.*** "The Olympian Council House and Council." *HSCP* 19 (1908): 1-60.

476. ***Dyer, Louis.*** "The Olympian Theatron." *JHS* 28, Part 2 (1908): 250-273.

477. ***Eckstein, F.*** *ANATHEMATA. Studien zu den Weigeschenken Strengen Stils im Heiligtum von Olympia.* Berlin: Mann, 1969.

478. ***Fellmann, Berthold, et al.*** *100 Jahre deutsche Ausgrabung in Olympia.* Munich, 1972. Catalogue for the exhibition during the Munich Olympics.

479. ***Gardiner, E. N.*** "The Origin of the Olympic Festival," Chapter 5 in *Olympia. Its History and Remains.* Pages 58-76. See no. 342.

480. ***Hampe, R.*** and ***Jantzen, U.*** "Die Grabung im Fruehjahr 1937." *Olympia Bericht.* 1936-1937: 25-97.

481. ***Harris, H. A.*** "An Olympic Epigram." *G&R* Ser. 2. 7 (1960): 3-8.

482. ***Herrmann, H. V.*** *Olympia - Heiligtum und Wettkampfstaette. 100 Jahre deutsche Ausgrabung in Olympia. Katalog der Ausstellung 1. 7. - 1. 10.* Munich, 1972.

483. ***Herrmann, H. V.*** *"Zanes." RE Suppl.* 14 (1974): col. 977ff.

484. ***Hyde, W. W.*** *Olympic Victor Monuments and Greek Athletic Art.* Washington, 1921.
Review: *AP* 1924-26: *BFC* 32: 60-62 Terzaghi. *AJPh*1924: 85-88 Shear.

485. ***Kunze, E.*** *Bericht von den Ausgrabungen in Olympia.* Berlin, 1956.

486. ***Kunze, E.*** and ***Schleif, H.***, eds. *Olympische Forschungen.* 12 vols. Berlin, 1944-1979.

487. ***Mallwitz, A.*** "Ein Jahrhundert deutsche Ausgrabungen in Olympia." *MDAI(A)* 92 (1977): 1ff.

488. ***Mallwitz, A.*** *Olympia und seine Bauten.* Munich, 1972.

489. ***Meyer, E.*** "Olympia 1. Topographie." *KP* 4 (1972): 279-284.

490. **Meyer, E.** "Pisa, Pisatis." *RE* 20, 2. Stuttgart, 1950: (1732) 1754-1755.

491. ***Meyer, E.*** "Pisa, Pisatis." *KP* 4 (1972): 866-867.

492. ***Regner, J.*** "Olympionikai." *RE* 18. Stuttgart, 1939: coll. 232-241.

493. ***Schleif, H.*** "Die Badeanlagen von Olympia." *F&F* 1942: 244-245.

494. ***Schoene, H.*** "Neue Angaben ueber den Hippodrom zu Olympia." *JDAI* 12 (1897): 150-160.

495. ***Semmlinger, L.*** *Weih-, Sieger-, und Ehreninschriften aus Olympia und seiner Umgebung.* Diss.: Erlangen-Nuremburg, 1974.

496. ***Wernicke, K.*** "Olympische Beitraege 4. Das Gymnasium. 5. Der Hippodrom." *JDAI* 9 (1894): 191-204.

497. ***Wiesner, J.*** "Olympia (Topographie und Geschichte der Monumente)." *RE* 18, 1. Stuttgart, 1939: coll. 71-174.

498. ***Wotschitzky, A.*** "Olympische Kampfstaetten." *Olympia einst und jetzt. Vortragsreihe der Universitaet Innsbruck und des Kulturamtes der Stadt Innsbruck aus Anlass der 9 Olympischen Winterspiele.* Schriftleit. Muth, R., Zusammenstell. des Bildteiles Wotschitzky, A. Innsbruck Selbstverl. des Stadtmagistrates, 1964: 21-36.

499. ***Yalouris, N.*** *Olympia. Altis und Museum.* Munich and Zurich, 1972.

IV

THE OTHER PANHELLENIC FESTIVALS

A. General

500. ***Brophy, R. H.*** "Deaths in the Panhellenic Games. Arrichion and Creugas." *AJPh* 99 (1978): 363-390.

501. ***Buhmann, H.*** *Der Sieg in Olympia und der anderen panhellenischen Spielen.* See no. 322.

502. ***Hanell, K.*** "Trieteris." *RE* 7 A, 1. Stuttgart, 1939: 122-124, nr. 1.

503. ***Klee, Theophil.*** *Zur Geschichte der gymnischen Agone an griechischen Festen.* Leipzig/Berlin, 1918. Reprint, Chicago: Ares, 1980.

504. ***Knab, R.*** *Die Periodoniken. Ein Beitrag zur Geschichte der gymnischen Agone an den vier griechischen Hauptfesten.* Diss.: Giessen Bottrop i. W. Postberg, 1934. Reprint, Chicago: Ares, 1980.

505. ***Krause, J. H.*** *Die Pythien, Nemeen, Isthmien.* Leipzig, 1841. (= Vol. 4 of idem, *Hellenica,* 4 vols, Leipzig, 1838-1841).

506. ***McGregor, M. F.*** "Cleisthenes of Sikyon and the Panhellenic Games." *TAPA* 72 (1941): 266-287.

507. ***Montgomery, H. C.*** *"Periodonîkes." RE* 19 Stuttgart, 1937: coll. 813-815.

508. ***Moretti, L.*** "Note sugli antichi Periodonikai." *Athenaeum* N. S. 32 (1954): 115-120.

509. ***Ziegler, K.*** "Trieteris." *KP* 5 (1975): 958 nr. 2.

B. Pythian

510. ***Aupert, P.*** and ***Callot, E.*** *Le Stade. Fouilles de Delphes.* vol. 2. Paris, 1979.

511. ***Ebert, J.*** *"Paides Pythikoî." Philologus* 109 (1965): 152-156.

512. ***Gaspar, C.*** and ***Pottier, E.*** "Pythia." *D.-S.* 4, 1. Paris, 1907: 784-794.

512a. ***Holmberg, E.*** *Delphi and Olympia.* Gottenburg, 1979.

513. ***Miller, S. G.*** "The Date of the First Pythiad." *CSCA* 11 (1979): 127-158.

514. ***Peek, W.*** "Delphische Gedichte." *MDAI(A)* 67 (1942): 232-269.

515. ***Pomtow, H.*** "Delphoi." *RE Suppl.* 4. Stuttgart, 1924: coll. 1189-1432.

516. *Pomtow, H.* "Studien zu den Weihgeschenken und der Topographie von Delphi." *MDAI(A)* 31 (1906): 437-563.
517. *Pomtow, H.* "Studien zu den Weihgeschenken und der Topographie von Delphi. 5." *Klio* 9 (1909): 153-193.
518. *Pottier, E.* "Pythia." *D.-S.* 4, 1. Paris, 1907: 784-794.
519. *Robert, L.* "Les boules dans les types monétaires agonistiques." *Hellenica* 7 (1949): 93-104.
520. *Roux, G.* "A propos des gymnases de Delphes et de Délos. Le site du Damatrion et le sens du mot sphairistérion." *BCH* 104 (1980): 127-149.
521. *Roux, G.* *Delphes, son oracle et ses dieux.* Paris: Belles Lettres, 1976.
522. *Ziegler, K.* "Pythionikai." *RE* 24, 1. Stuttgart, 1963: 563-564.
523. *Ziegler, K.* "Pythionikai." *KP* 4 (1972): 1277.

C. Isthmian

524. *Angeli, Bernardini, P.* "Una nouva fonte sull'istituzione dei giochi istmici (P. Oxy. 2451 fr. 1)." *QUCC* 16 (1973): 138-141.
525. *Biers, W. R.* and *Geagan, D. J.* "A New List of the Victors in the Caesarea at Isthmia." *Hesperia* 39 (1970): 79-93.
526. *Broneer, O.* "Excavations at Isthmia 1959-1961." *Hesperia* 31 (1962): 1-25.
527. *Broneer, O.* "Excavations at Isthmia, Fourth Campaign, 1957-1958." *Hesperia* 28 (1959): 298-343.
528. *Broneer, O.* "Excavations at Isthmia, Third Campaign, 1955-1956." *Hesperia* 27 (1958): 1-37.
529. *Broneer, O.* "Excavations at Isthmia 1959-60." *Hesperia* 35, No. 1 (1962):
530. *Broneer, O.* *Isthmia I; Temple of Poseidon.* Princeton, Amer. School of Class. Stud. at Athens, 1971.
531. *Broneer, O.* *Isthmia II; Topography and Architecture.* Princeton, Amer. School of Class. Studies at Athens, 1973.
532. *Broneer, O.* "Isthmia, its Gods and Games." *Olympic Academy* (1971): 164-169.
533. *Broneer, O.* "Isthmiaca. Investigations at the Site of the Isthmian Games." *Klio* 39 (1961): 249-270.
534. *Broneer, O.* "The Isthmian Games and the Sanctuary of Poseidon." *Greek Heritage* 1, No. 4 (1964) 42-49.
535. *Broneer, O.* "The Isthmian Victory Crown." *AJA* 66 (1962): 259-263.

536. ***Broneer, O.*** "The Later Stadium at Isthmia." Summary *AJA* 64 (1965): 166.

536a. ***Broneer, O.***, "Paul and the Pagan Cults at Isthmia," *Harvard Theological Review* 64 (1971): 169-187.

537. ***Couve, L.*** "Isthmia." *D.-S.* 3, 1. Paris, 1900: 588-591.

538. ***Daux, G.*** "Décret d'Ephèse pour un vanqueur aux Isthme et aux Nemea." *ZPE* 28 (1978): 41-47.

539. ***Dunst, G.*** "Die Inschrift des Periodoniken Leon." *ZPE* 3 (1968): 139-148. cf. R. Mellor "The Athletic Leon Once Again," no. 827.

539a. ***Jordan, D. R.***, and ***Spawforth, J. S.***, "A New Document from the Isthmian Games," *Hesperia* 51 (1982): 65-68.

539b. ***Kent, J. H.***, *Corinth* VIII.3 (Princeton, 1966). Agonistic inscriptions: 149-191 and 208-230.

540. ***Krause, J. H.*** *Die Pythien, Nemeen, Isthmien.* See no. 505.

540a. ***Meritt, B. D.***, *Corinth* VIII.1 (Cambridge, Mass., 1931). Agonistic inscriptions: 14-20.

541. ***Reinmuth, O. W.*** "Isthmien." *KP* 2 (1967): col. 1475.

542. ***Schneider K.*** "Isthmia." *RE* 9, 2. Stuttgart, 1916: coll. 2248-2255.

542a. ***West, A. B.***, *Corinth* VIII.2 (Cambridge, Mass., 1931).

D. Nemean

543. ***Blegen, C. W.*** "The American Excavation at Nemea." *Art and Archaeology* 19 (1925): 175ff; and in *AJA* 31 (1927): 421 ff.

544. ***Blegen, C. W.*** "The December Excavations at Nemea." *Art and Archaeology* 22 (1926): 127-134 and 139.

545. ***Blegen, C. W.*** "Excavations at Nemea 1926." *AJA* 2nd Series 31, No. 4 (1942): 421-440.

546. ***Bradeen, D. W.*** "Inscriptions from Nemea." *Hesperia* 35, No. 4 (1966): 320-330.

547. ***Daux, G.*** "Décret d'Ephèse pour un vanquer aux Isthme e aux Nemea." See no. 538.

548. ***Gaspar, C.*** "Nemea." *D.-S.* 4, 1. Paris, 1907: 50-52.

549. ***Hanell, K.*** "Nemea 4." *RE* 16, 2. Stuttgart, 1935: coll. 2322-2327.

550. ***Hart, Dale P.*** "The Ancient Nemean Festival." *Canadian Journal of Sport and Physical Education* 8, 2 (1977): 24-34.

551. ***Miller, S. G.*** "Excavations at Nemea 1973-1974." *Hesperia* 44 (1975): 143-172.

552. ***Miller, S. G.*** "Excavations at Nemea 1975." *Hesperia* 45 (1976): 174-202.

553. ***Miller, S. G.*** "Excavations at Nemea 1976." *Hesperia* 46 (1977): 1-26.

554. ***Miller, S. G.*** "Excavations at Nemea 1977." *Hesperia* 47 (1978): 58-88.

555. ***Miller, S. G.*** "Excavations at Nemea 1978." *Hesperia* 48 (1979): 73-103.

556. ***Miller, S. G.*** "The Pentathlon for Boys at Nemea." See no. 801.

557. ***Miller, S. G.*** "Tunnel Vision: The Nemean Games." *Archaeology* 33 (1980): 54-56.

558. ***Reinmuth, O. W.*** "Nemea." *KP* 4 (1972): col. 47.

559. ***Romano, D. G.*** "An Early Stadium at Nemea." *Hesperia* 46 (1977): 27-31.

V

LOCAL GAMES

A. The Panathenaic Festival

560. ***Brauchitsch, G.*** *Die panathenaeischen Preisamphoren.* Leipzig and Berlin: B. G. Teubner, 1910.

561. ***Broneer, O.*** "Notes on Three Athenian Cult Places." *AE* 1960 (1965): 54-67.

562. ***Davison, J. A.*** "Notes on the Panathenaea." *JHS* 78 (1958): 23-42.

563. ***Deubner, L.*** *Attische Feste.* Darmstadt: Wissenschaftlische Buchgesellschaft, 1956 repr. of Berlin: Keller, 1932. Second edition by Doer, B. Berlin Akad.-Verl., 1966.[2]

Reviews: AP 1933: *DLZ* (1933): 1969-1974 Nilsson. *REA* (1933): 341 Roussel. *JHS* (1933): 146-148. *HZ* 149: 102 Kern.

564. ***Dickins, G.*** "The Hieron of Athena Chalkioikos." *ABSA* 13 (1906-1907): 137-154.

565. ***Gardiner, E. N.*** "Panathenaic Amphorae." *JHS* 32 (1912): 179-193.

566. ***Gardner, P.*** "Boat-races at Athens." *JHS* 2 (1881): 315-317.

567. ***Giglioli, C. Q.*** "La corsa della fiaccola ad Atene." *RAL* 31 (1922): 315-335.

568. ***Girard, P.*** *L'éducation athénienne.* See no. 47.

569. ***Juethner, J.*** *"Euandrías agon." RE* 6, 1. Stuttgart, 1907: col. 839.

569a. ***Kyle, D.*** *A Historical Study of Athletics in Ancient Athens.* Ph. D. Diss., McMaster, 1982. *DA* 42.9 4101-A.

570. ***Meritt, B. D.*** "Greek Inscriptions." *Hesperia* 32, No. 1 (1963): 1-56. Regarding panathenaic festival.

571. ***Meritt, B. D.*** "Greek Inscriptions." *Hesperia* 15, No. 3 (1946): 210-268. Regarding victory at the Panathenaia.

572. ***Mommsen, A.*** *Feste der Stadt Athen im Altertum.* Leipzig: B. G. Teubner, 1898: 61ff.

573. ***Nagy, Blaise.*** "The Athenian Athlothetai." *GRBS* 19, No. 4 (Winter 1978): 307-313.

574. ***Peters, K.*** *Studien zu den panathenaeischen Preisamphoren.* Diss., Cologne, Kunst des Altertums II. Berlin: de Gruyter, 1942.

Reviews: AP 1942-44: *MPh* 50 (1943): 187 van Hoorn. *PhW* 144: 175-180 Lippold.

575. ***Preuner, E.*** "Amphiaraia und Panathenaia." *Hermes* 57 (1922): 80-106.

576. ***Thompson, H. A.*** "The Panathenaic Festival." *AA* 1961: col. 224-231.

577. ***Tiberios, M. A.*** *"PANATHENA-I-KA." AD* 29 (1974): 142ff.

578. ***Ziehen, L.*** "Panathenaia." *RE* 18, 3. Stuttgart, 1949: coll. 457-493.

B. Other Local Games

579. ***Angeli, Bernardini, P.*** "Le Halieia di Rodi." *Stadion* 3 (1977): 1-3.

580. ***Angeli, Bernardini, P.*** "Hekatombeia o Heraia di Argo." *Stadion* 2 (1976): 213-217.

581. ***Bethe, E.*** "Amphiaria." *RE* 1, 2. Stuttgart, 1894: coll. 1885-1886.

582. ***Broneer, O.*** "Hero Cults in the Corinthian Agora." *Hesperia* 11, No. 2 (1942): 128-161.

583. ***Couve, L.*** "Hermaia." *D.-S.* 3, 1. Paris, 1896: 134-135.

584. ***Daux, G.*** "Sur quelques inscriptions (anthroponymes, concours à Pergame, serment éphébique)." *REG* 84 (1971): 350-383 (365-369 on Pergamon).

585. ***Decker, W.*** "Bemerkungen zum Agon fuer Antinoos in Antinoupolis (Antinoeia)." *KBSW* 2 (1973): 38-56.

586. ***Deubner, L.*** *Attische Feste.* See no. 563.

587. ***Diem, C.*** "Sportfest auf Sizilien aus alter Zeit." *Olympische Rundschau* H. 19 (1942): 12-20 (=*Olympische Flamme* 2: 586-593).

588. ***Diem, C.*** "Une fête sportive en Sicile dans l'Antiquité." *Olympische Rundschau* 20 (1942): 36-41.

589. ***Dow, S.*** "Athletic Agones in Roman Athens Honoring Tykhe Poleos." *AJA* 100 (1979): 31-44.

590. ***Dunst, G.*** "Die Siegerliste der samischen Heraia." *ZPE* 1 (1967): 225-239.

591. ***Foucart, P.*** "Basileia." *D.-S.* 1, 1. Paris, 1877: 677.

592. ***Frel, J.*** "Games on the Rhodian Shore." *AAA* 8 (1975): 77-78.

593. ***Geagen, D. J.*** "Notes of the Agonistic Institutions of Roman Corinth." *GRBS* 9, No. 1 (1968): 69-80.

594. ***Gerassimov, T.*** "Remarques sur les jeux pythiques, Alexandrins et kendrises à Philippopolis." (in Bulgarian) *Studia in honorem D. Decev.* Sofia Acad. des Sciences de Bulgarie, 1958: 289-304. Cf. German resumé in *BCO* 5 (1960): 136.
Review of Mélange: AP 1960: *LF* 7 (1959): 307 Vidman.

595. ***Heberdey, R.*** "Gymnische und andere Agone in Termessus Pisidiae." *Anatolian Studies presented to Sir W. M. Ramsay.* Buckler, W. H. and Calder, W. M., eds. Manchester: The University Press, London, and New York: Longmans, Green & Co., 1923.
596. ***Humpherys, S. C.*** "The Nothoi of Kynosarges." *JHS* 94 (1974): 88-95.
597. ***Kadletz, E.*** "The Race and Procession of the Athenian *Oscophoroi." GRBS* 21 (1980): 363-371.
598. ***Kontorini, V. N.*** "Les concours des grands Éréthimia à Rhodes." *BCH* 99 (1975): 97-117.
599. ***Kublanow, M. M.*** "Agone und agonistische Festveranstaltungen in der antiken Staedten der noerdlichen Schwarzmeerkueste." *Altertum* 5/6 (1959/1960): 131-148.
600. ***Laemmer, M.*** "Griechische Wettkaempfe in Galilaee unter der Herrschaft der Herodes Antipas." *KBSW* 5 (1976): 37-67.
601. ***Laemmer, M.*** "Griechische Wettkaempfe in Jerusalem und ihre politischen Hintergruende." *KBSW* 2 (1973): 182-227.
602. ***Laemmer, M.*** *Olympien und Hadrianeen im antiken Ephesos.* Koeln Hist. Semin. der Dt. Sporthochschule, 1967.
603. ***Maróti, E.*** "Zum roemerzeitlichen Weiterleben des Theognis." *AAntHung* 15 (1967): 153-158. (=Theognis vers egy császárkori feliraton. *MTAI* 1. *Oszt. Koezl.* 24 (1967): 91-95).
604. ***Masow, H. von.*** "Die stele des Ainetos in Amyklai." *MDAI(A)* 51 (1926): 41-47.
605. ***Merkelbach, R.*** "Ueber ein ephesisches Dekret fuer einen Athleten aus Aphrodisias und ueber den Athletentitel *parádoxos." ZPE* 14 (1974): 91-96.
606. ***Mitsos, M.*** "Eine agonistische Inschrift aus Argos." *MDAI(A)* 65 (1940): 47-56.
607. ***Mommsen, A.*** *Feste der Stadt Athen im Altertum.* See no. 572.
608. ***Piernavieja, Rozitis P.*** "Dos notas sobre los antiguos ludi espanoles." 12 Congresso nacional de arqueología, Jaén 1971: Zaragoza Semin. de arqueol., 1973: 579-582.
609. ***Pouilloux, J.*** "Un athlète nouveau au gymnase Salamine de Chypre." *RA* (1971): 291-294.
610. ***Preuner, E.*** "Amphiaria und Panathenaia." See no. 575.
611. ***Rigsby, K. J.*** "Sacred Ephebic Games at Oxyrhynchus." See no. 311.
612. ***Ringwood, Irene C.*** *Agonistic Features of Local Greek Festivals Chiefly from Inscriptional Evidence I.* Diss.: Columbia Univ., 1927.
613. ***Ringwood-Arnold, Irene C.*** "Agonistic Festivals in Italy and Sicily." *AJA* 64 (1960): 245-251.

614. ***Ringwood-Arnold, Irene C.*** "Festivals of Ephesus." *AJA* 69 (1965): 17-22.

615. ***Ringwood-Arnold, Irene C.*** "Festivals of Rhodes." *AJA* 40 (1936): 432-436.

616. ***Ringwood-Arnold, Irene C.*** "Local Festivals at Delos." *AJA* 37, No. 3 (1933): 452-458.

617. ***Ringwood-Arnold, Irene C.*** "Local Festivals of Euboea, Chiefly from Inscriptional Evidence." *AJA* 33, No. 3 (1929): 385-392.

618. ***Ringwood-Arnold, Irene C.*** "The Shield of Argos." *AJA* 41 (1937): 436-440.

619. ***Robert, L.*** "Deux inscriptions agonistiques de Rhodes." *AE* (1966 (1968)): 108-118.

620. ***Robert, L.*** "Inscriptions agonistiques. Hiérocesarée, nr. 6-13." *Hellenica* 6 (1948): 43-48.

621. ***Robert, L.*** "Inscription agonistique d'Ancyre. Concours d'Ancyre." *Hellenica* 11-12 (1953-1954): 350-568.

622. ***Robert, L.*** "Inscription agonistique de Smyrne." *Hellenica* 7 (1949): 105-113.

623. ***Robert, L.*** "Monnaies et concours de Laodicée du Lykos." *Hellenica* 7 (1949): 89-92.

624. ***Robert, L.*** "Sur les inscriptions de Chios 3. Inscription agonistique." *BCH* 57 (1933): 539-543 (= *OMS* 1: 507-511.)

625. ***Robert, L.*** "Sur une inscription agonistique de Thespies." *Hellenica* 2 (1946): 5-14.

626. ***Robert, L.*** "Un athlète Milésien." *Hellenica* 7 (1949): 117-125.

627. ***Robinson, E. S. G.*** "Rhegion, Zankle-Messana and the Samians." *JHS* 66 (1946): 13-20.

628. ***Saglio, E.*** "Chalkeia." *D.-S.* 1, 2. Paris, 1887: 1098.

629. ***Schneider, C.*** *Kulturgeschichte des Hellenismus.* Munich: Beck, 1969: vol. 2, 190-198.

Reviews: AP 1969: *CR* 19 (1969): 69-72 Murray. *CJ* 64 (1969): 230-231 Wassermann. *JHS* 89 (1969): 176-177 Ehrenberg. *Gymnasium* 76 (1969): 143-144 Bayer. *LEC* 37 (1969): 416-417 Wankenne. *BO* 26 (1969): 457. AP 1970: *AAHG* 22 (1969): 183-186 Hampl. *Gnomon* 42 (1970): 469-480 Luck. *II Gymnasium* 77 (1970): 441-442 Bayer. *CW* 63 (1970): 306 Edinger. *RecSR* 58 (1970): 461-462 Vallin. *AC* 39 (1970): 670-673 Laronde.

630. ***Searls, H. E.*** and ***Dinsmoor, W. B.*** "The Date of the Olympian Heraeum." *AJA* 49, No. 1 (1945): 62-80.

631. ***Tréheux, J.*** "Études d'épigraphie Délienne." *BCH* 76 (1952): 562-595.

632. ***Wiseman, J.*** "Excavations at Corinth, the Gymnasium Area, 1965." *Hesperia* 36 (1967): 13-41. 402-428.

633. ***Wiseman, J.*** "The Gymnasium Area at Corinth 1969-70." *Hesperia* 41, No. 1 (1972): 1-42.

VI

THE GREEK EVENTS

A. Running

634, *Allison, F. G.* "The Original Marathon Runner." *CW* 24 (1930-31): 152.

635. *Bayr, G.* "Ueber den Schnellauf der Hellenen. Eine Klarstellung." *Die Leibesuebungen* 5 (1929): 353.

636. *Beazley, J. D.* "A Hoplitodromos Cup." *ABSA* 46 (1951): 7-15.

637. *Bengston, H.* "Aus der Lebensgeschichte eines griechischen Distanzlaeufers." *Symbolae Osloenses* 32 (1956): 35-39.

638. *Biliński, B. L'antico oplite-corridore di Maratona. Leggenda o realtà.* Conf. tenuta all'Accad. Polacca di Roma 1959 Accad. Pol. Bibl. di Roma Conf. 8. Rome: Signorelli, 1960.

639. *Biliński, B.* "L'hémérodrome Philonidès, son record et la nouvelle inscription d'Aigion." *Eos* 50, 1 (1959, 1960): 69-80.

640. *Broneer, O.* "Starting Devices in Greek Stadia." *AJA* 76 (1972): 205-206.

641. *Bussemaker.* "Cursus." *D.-S.* 1, 2. Paris, 1887: 1643-1645.

642. *Bussemaker.* "Hemerodromoi." *D.-S.* 3, 1. Paris, 1896: 71.

643. *Defradas, J.* "Sur l'interprétation de la deuxième Olympique de Pindare." *REG* 84 (1971): 131-143.

644. *Diem, C. Der Laufer von Marathon.* Leipzig, 1941.

645. *Diem, C.* "Hat es den Laufer von Marathon gegeben?" *Olympische Flamme* 2: 580-583.

646. *Eitrem, S.* "Koroibos." *RE* 11, 2. Stuttgart, 1922: 1420-1421, nr. 2.

647. *Gardiner, E. N.* "Notes on the Greek Footrace." *JHS* 23 (1903): 261-291.

648. *Gruendel, L. Die Darstellung des Laufens in der griechischen Kunst.* Diss.: Wuerzburg, 1934.

649. *Gruendel, L.* "Haben die Griechen den Passlauf gepflegt?" *Die Leibesuebungen* 6 (1930): 631-635.

650. *Hueppe, W.* "Die Legende vom Marathonlauf." *LKE* 54 (1935): 142-143.

651. *Hultsch.* "Diaulos 3." *RE* 5, 1. Stuttgart, 1903: coll. 354-355.

652. ***Hyde, W. W.*** "The Marathon Race." *CW* 27 (1943-44): 166-167.

653. ***Jachowski, H.*** "Die Bedeutung des Laufes in der Antike." *Die Leibeserziehung* (1963): 281-286, 323-328.

654. ***Juethner, J.*** *"Diaulos 2."* *RE* 5, 1. Stuttgart, 1903: col. 354.

655. ***Juethner, J.*** *"Dolichos 4."* *RE* 5, 1. Stuttgart, 1903: coll. 1282-1283.

656. ***Juethner, J.*** *"Dromos* 2." *RE* 5, 2. Stuttgart, 1905: coll. 1717-1720.

657. ***Juethner, J.*** *"Hemerodromos."* *RE* 8, 1. Stuttgart, 1912: coll. 232-233.

657a. ***Juethner, J.*** "Hippios 5." *RE* 8, 2. Stuttgart, 1913: coll. 1719-1720.

658. ***Juethner, J.*** *Die athletischen Leibesuebungen der Griechen. II. Einzelne Sportarten: 1. Lauf-, Sprung-, und Wurfbewerbe.* Brien, F., ed. *SAWW* 249, 2. Wien: Boehlau, 1968.

Reviews: AP 1971: *CR* 21 (1971): 84-86 Harris. *AJA* 75 (1971): 101-102 Broneer.

659. ***Juethner, J.*** "Stadion (Lauf)." *RE* 3 A, 2. Stuttgart, 1929: coll. 1963-1966.

660. ***Kirchner, J.*** "Astylos." *RE* 2, 2. Stuttgart, 1898: 1869, nr. 3.

661. ***Kirchner, J.*** "Dromeus." *RE* 5, 2. Stuttgart, 1905.: 1714, nr. 2.

662. ***Kiss, M.*** "Ókori távgyaloglás." ("Pedestrianism in Antiquity.") *Herkules* 10 (1893): 42-43.

663. ***Lenschau, Th.*** "Ladas." *RE* 12, 1. Stuttgart, 1924: 380, nr. 1.

664. ***Lucas, J. A.*** "A History of the Marathon-race 490 B.C. to 1975." *JSH* 3 (1976): 120-138.

665. ***Matthews, V. J.*** "The Hemerodromoi. Ultra Long-distance Running in Antiquity." *CW* 68 (1974): 161-169.

666. ***Merkelbach, R.*** *"Poiésas súndromon."* *ZPE* 11 (1973): 128-130.

667. ***Mezö, F.*** "A marathoni csata és a marathonfutás." ("The Battle of Marathon and the Marathon Run.") *Testnevelés* 6 (1953): 647-656.

668. ***Miller, S.*** "Turns and Lanes in the Ancient Stadium." *AJA* 84 (1980): 159-166.

669. ***Miltner, Fr.*** "Oibotas." *RE* 17, 2. Stuttgart, 1937: 2096.

670. ***Moestue, W.*** "Die griechische Ablaufbezirk." *Die Leibesuebungen* 9 (1933): 25-28.

671. ***Moestue, W.*** "Griechische Ablaufstellung und Ablaufvorgaenge." *HfL* 11 (1939): 415-417.

672. ***Moestue, W.*** "Die griechische Laufbahnen." *Deutsche Turnzeitung* (1932): 1085ff.

673. ***Moetsue, W.*** "Mallinien, Wendeschranken und Zielbezirke im griechischen Stadion." *LKE* 52 (1933): 291-294.

674. ***Neumann, G.*** "Der Waffenlauf im antiken Griechenland- Schriftliche Quellen und bildliche Ueberlieferung." *Der Tuebinger Waffenlaeufer.* Hausmann, U., ed. Tuebinger Studien zur Archaeologie und Kunstgeschichte 4. Tuebingen: Wasmuth, 1977: 31ff.

675. ***Niese, B.*** "Chionis." *RE* 3, 2. Stuttgart, 1899: 2286, nr. 1.

676. ***Obst.*** "Ladas." *RE* 12, 1. Stuttgart, 1924: 380-381, nr. 2.

677. ***Raubitschek, A.*** "Phanas." *RE* 19, 2. Stuttgart, 1938: coll. 1759-1760.

678. ***Reinmuth, O. W.*** *"Diaulos." KP* 1 (1964): 1517-1518.

679. ***Reinmuth, O. W.*** *"Dolichos." KP* 2 (1967): 116.

680. ***Reisch, E.*** *"Apheteria." RE* 1, 2. Stuttgart, 1894: coll. 2717-2718.

681. ***Reisch, E.*** *"Balbis." RE* 2, 2. Stuttgart, 1896: col. 2819.

682. ***Robert, L.*** "Un vainqueur aux Hyakinthotropia." *Hellenica* 7 (1949): 114-116.

683. ***Roos, P.*** "The Start of the Greek Foot-race." *Opuscula Atheniensia* 6 (1965): 149-156.

684. ***Suolahti, J.*** "The Origin of the Story about the First Marathonrunner." *Arctos* 5 (1967): 127-133.

685. ***Wirt, G.*** *"Dromos." KP* 2 (1967): 1165.

B. Torch Race

686. ***Ashmole, B.*** "Torch-Racing at Rhamnus." *AJA* 66 (1962): 233-234.

687. ***Ebert, J.*** "Zu Fackellaeufen und anderen Problemen in einer griechischen agonistischen Inschrift aus Aegypten." *Stadion* 5 (1979): 1ff.

688. ***Giglioli, G. Q.*** "La corsa della fiaccola ad Atene." See no. 567.

689. ***Giglioli, G. Q.*** "Lampadedromia." *Archaeologia Classica* 3 (1951): 147-162.

690. ***Giglioli, G. Q.*** "La lampadedromia in due recentissime publicazioni." *ArchClass* 4 (1952): 94-97.

691. ***Juenthner, J.*** *"Lampadedromia." RE* 12, 1. Stuttgart, 1924: coll. 569-577.

692. ***Martin, A.*** *"Lampadedromia." D.-S.* 3, 2. Paris, 1904: 909-914.

693. ***Pouilloux, J.*** "Lampadédromies thasiennes." *Mélanges d'Archéologie et d'Histoire Charles Picard.* Paris, 1949: 847-857.

694. *Sterett, J.R.S.* "The Torch Race." *AJA* 22, No. 88 (1901): 406.
695. *Volkmann, H.* *"Lampadedromia."* *KP* 3 (1969): 467-468.

C. Jumping

696. *Ackermann, A. S. E.* "The Long Jump in Ancient Greece." *Notes and Queries* 171 (1936): 47-48, 83, 101-102.
697. *Diem, C.* "Vom Sprung der Alten." (in German and English) *Olympische Rdsch.*, 1939, 6: 16-19.
698. *Gardiner, E. N.* "Further Notes on the Greek Jump." *JHS* 24 (1904): 179-194.
699. *Gardiner, E. N.* "Phayllus and His Record Jump." *JHS* 24 (1904): 70-80.
700. *Guarducci, M.* "Tre iscrizioni arcaiche di Corintho. 3. L'altere dell'Istmo." *ASAA* 21-22 (1959-1960): 284-287.
701. *Harris, H. A.* "An Olympic Epigram. The Athletic Feats of Phayllos." *G&R* 7 (1960): 3-8.
702. *Howland, R. L.* "Phayllus and the Long-jump Record." (Anth. Pal. Append. 297.) *PCPhS* 181 (1950-1951): 31.
703. *Hyde, W. W.* "The Pentathlon Jump." *AJPh* 59 (1938): 405-417.
704. *Juethner, J.* *"Halma."* *RE* 7, 2. Stuttgart, 1912: col. 2273-2276.
705. *Juethner, J.* *"Halter."* *RE* 7, 2. Stuttgart, 1912: coll. 2284-2285.
706. *Juethner, J.* *"Halterobolía."* *RE* 7, 2. Stuttgart, 1912: coll. 2285-2286.
707. *Juethner, J.* *Die Athletischen Leibesuebungen II.* See no. 658.
708. *Juethner, J.* "Der Phayllossprung." *Bull. Offic. du Comité Internat. Olymp.* 44 (1940): 3-4.
709. *Juethner, J.* *"Skámma."* *RE* 3 A, 1. Stuttgart, 1927: coll. 435-437.
710. *Juethner, J.* "Die zylinderrischen Halteren." *MDAI(R)* 43 (1928): 13-18.
711. *Klincsek, J.* "Az ugrás szerepe az ókorban (Francia forrásból.)" ("The Role of Jumping in Antiquity.") *Tornaügy* 4 (1886-87): 15-16 (K. jelzéssel.)
712. *Kueppers, W.* "Phayllossprung." *AA* 1900: 104-106.
713. *Latte, K.* "De saltationibus Graecorum capita quinque." *Religionsgeschichtliche Versuche und Vorarbeiten* 13 (1913) Berlin: De Gruyter, 1967, reprint.
714. *Legrand, Ph. E.* *"Saltus."* *D.-S.* 4, 2. Paris, 1907: 1045-1046.
715. *Lindner, E.* "Die Benutzung der Halteren im Weitsprung der Antike." *AA* 1956: 128-130.

716. *Lindner, E.* *Der Halterensprung, eine Deutung der griechischen Wettkampfuebung.* Diss: Marburg, 1955.

717. *Mezö, F.* "16 méter 94 cm. (Phayllos távolugrása a 75. olympis korában.)." ("Sixteen meters and thirty four centimeters: the Broadjump of Phayllos in the Seventy-fifth Olympiad.") *Testnevelés-Sport* 1 (1926): 6. sz: 168-171.

718. *Mezö, F.* "Az ókori távolugrás." ("The Broadjump of Antiquity.") *Testnevelés* 14 (1941): 1-22.

719. *Mezö, F.* "Das Raetsel des altgriechischen Weitsprungs." *Altertum* 6 (1958): 165-172.

720. *Porzsolt, L.* "Az ókori ugrás." ("The Jump in Antiquity.") *Herkules* 2 (1895): 25. sz. 4.

721. *Reinmuth, O. W.* "*Halter.*" *KP* 2 (1967): 927.

722. *Reisch, E.* "*Balbís.*" See no. 681.

723. *Reisch, E.* "*Batér.*" *RE* 3, 1. Stuttgart, 1897: coll. 122-123.

724. *Ridder, A. de.* "*Halter.*" *D.-S.* 3, 1. Paris, 1899: 5-7.

725. *Stier, H. E.* "Phayllos 2." *RE* 19, 2. Stuttgart, 1939: coll. 1903-1904.

726. *Téry, O.* "Az ugrás szerepe az ókorban." ("The Role of the Jump in Antiquity.") *Tornaügy* 4 (1886-87): 5-15.

D. Discus Throwing

727. *Bellugne, P.* "Le lancement du disque dans l'antiquité." *GBA* Jg. 78. vol. 16. (1936): 69-82.

728. *Blumenthal, A.* "Zur Technik des antiken Diskuswerfs." *Die Leibeserziehung* (1968): 182-188.

729. *Castiglione, L.* "Die Diskobolia - ein Agarritus?" *AAnt-Hung* 15 (1967): 409-415.

730. *Chryssafis, J. C.* "Altgriechisches Diskuswerfen." *Vierteljahrschr. f. Koerperliche Erziehung* 3 (1907): 1.

731. *Chryssafis, J. C.* *Altgriechisches Diskuswerfen.* Athens, 1928.

732. *Decker, W.* "Zum Ursprung des Diskuswerfens." *Stadion* 2 (1976): 196-212.

733. *Dihl, M.* "Zum Diskobol des Myron." *Die Leibesuebungen* 2 (1926): 545-548.

734. *Gardiner, E. N.* "Throwing the Diskos." *JHS* 27 (1907): 1-36.

735. *Hoyer, F.* *Der Diskowerf nach kinematographischen Aufnahmen.* Diss.: Hamberg, 1936.

736. *Jakobsthal, J. P.* *Diskoi: WPrBerlin* no. 93. Berlin: de Gruyter, 1933.

737. ***Juethner, J.*** *"Diskobolia." RE* 5, 1. Stuttgart, 1903: coll. 1187-1188.

738. ***Juethner, J.*** *"Diskoi." JOeAI* 29 (1939): 32-43.

739. ***Juethner, J.*** *"Diskos 2." RE* 5, 1. Stuttgart, 1903: coll. 1188-1189.

740. ***Juethner, J.*** "Der homerische Diskos." *Festschrift Benndorf* 1898: 11ff.

741. ***Juethner, J.*** *Die athletischen Leibesuebungen II.* Se no. 658.

742. ***Juethner, J.*** "Das problem des myronischen Diskobols." *Oesterr. Jahresh.* 24 (1929): 123-161.

743. ***Kietz, G.*** *Agonistische Studien. 1. Der Diskuswerf bei den Griechen und seine kuenstlerischen Motive.* Phil. Diss.: Munich, 1862.

744. ***Kiss, I.*** "Az ógrörög diszkoszvetö stīlusa." ("The Style of the Ancient Greek Discus Thrower.") *Testnevelés* 16 (1943): 125-126.

745. ***Kiss, I.*** "Az ógörög diszkoszvetés." ("The Discus Throw in Ancient Greece.") *Testneveléstudomány* 1956: 240ff.

746. ***Pernice, E.*** "Zum Diskowerf." *JDAI* 23 (1908): 94-100.

747. ***Reisch, E.*** *"Balbis."* See no. 681.

748. ***Saglio, E.*** *"Discus." D.-S.* 2, 1. Paris, 1892: 277-280.

749. ***Schroeder, B.*** "Neues vom Diskowerfen." *AA* 1920: 61-84.

750. ***Schroeder, B.*** *Zum Diskobol des Myron.* Strassburg, 1913.

751. ***Schroeder, B.*** "Zur Technik des Diskuswerfens." *BJ* 123 (1915).

752. ***Schweitzer, B.*** "Der Diskowerfer der Glyptothek in Muenchen." See no. 1386.

753. ***Sieveking, J.*** "Der Myronische Diskobols." *Kunstkronik* 1917: 465-469.

754. ***Sieveking, J.*** "Zum Myronischen Diskobol." *PhW* (1922): 167-168.

755. ***Sümeghy, V.*** "Myron és a müncheni diszkosvetö szobrocska." ("Myron and the Miniature Sculpture of a Discus Thrower in Munich.") *AT* 5 (1958): 67-72.

756. ***Sümeghy, V.*** "Das Problem des Myronischen Diskobol." *Atti del settimo Congresso internazionale di Archeologia classica, Roma-Napoli 6-13 sett., 1958.* Rome: L'Erma, 1961 I: 281-285.

757. ***Sunowsky, R.*** *Die Darstellung des antiken Scheibenwurfes.* Diss.: Wien, 1939.

758. ***Uhlig, M.*** "Zum Diskuswerfer des Myron." *Die Leibesuebungen* 2 (1927): 357-361.

759. ***Zingerle, J.*** "Der Steinwurf des Bybon." *Commentationes Vindobonenses* 2 (1936): 111f.

E. Javelin Throwing

760. ***Ballester, Tormo, I.*** "El *amentum* en los vasos de San Miguel de Liria." *AEAA* 46 (1942): 48-53.
761. ***Domaszewski, A. von.*** *"Amentum."* *RE* 1, 2. Stuttgart, 1894: coll. 2901-2902.
762. ***Droysen, J. G.*** *"Akonistaí."* *RE* 1. Stuttgart, 1893: coll. 1185-1186.
763. ***Gardiner, E. N.*** "Throwing the Javelin." *JHS* 27 (1907): 249-273.
764. ***Harris, H. A.*** "Greek Javelin Throwing." *G&R* N. S. 10 (1963): 26-36.
765. ***Juethner, J.*** *"Akóniton-akonití."* *Glotta* 29 (1914): 73-77.
766. ***Juethner, J.*** *Die athletischen Leibesuebungen II.* See No. 658.
767. ***Lee, H. M.*** "The *térma* and the Javelin in Pindar. Nemean vii. 70-3, and Greek Athletics." *JHS* 96 (1976): 70-79.
768. ***Mezö, F.*** "Az ókori gerelyvetés." ("The Ancient Javelin Throw.") *Testenevelés* 3 (1930): 885-886.
769. ***Moestue, W.*** "Die Frage der griechischen Ablauf-Speerschranken. Eine kritische Studie." *HfL* 11 (1932): 375-377.
770. ***Neumann, A. R.*** *"Ammentum."* *KP* 1: 302.
771. ***Reisch, E.*** *"Akonití."* *RE* 1, 1. Stuttgart, 1893: coll. 1183-1185.
772. ***Reisch, E.*** *"Akontion 2."* *RE* 1, 1. Stuttgart, 1893: coll. 1183-1185.
773. ***Reisch, E.*** *"Balbís."* See no. 681.
774. ***Ridder, A. de.*** *"Jaculum."* *D.-S.* 3, 1. Paris, 1899: 594-602.
775. ***Saglio, E.*** *"Am(m)entum."* *D.-S.* 1, 1. Paris, 1877: 226-227.
776. ***Schneider, K.*** *"Harpastum."* *RE* 7, 2. Stuttgart, 1912: coll. 2405-2407.
777. ***Schulten, A.*** *"Pilum."* *RE,* Erste Reihe 20, 2 (1950): 1333-1369.

F. The Pentathlon

778. ***Bean, G. E.*** "Victory in the Pentathlon." *AJA* 60 (1956): 361-368.
779. ***Brein, F.*** "Die Wertung im Pentathlon." *Forschung und Funde. Festschrift Bernhard Neutsch.* Innsbruck: Institut fuer Sprachwissenschaft der Universitaet Innsbruck, 1980: 89-93.

780. *Ebert, J.* "Noch einmal zum Sieg im Pentathlon." *ZPE* 13 (1974): 257-262.

781. *Ebert, J. Zum Pentathlon der Antike. Untersuchungen ueber das System der Siegerermittlung und der Ausfuehrung des Halterensprunges.* Abh. der Akad. Wiss. zu Leipzig 56, 1. Berlin: Akad.-Verl., 1963.

Reviews: AP 1966: *Erasmus* 18 (1966): 378-380 Bloch. *DLZ* 87 (1966): 494-497 Rudolph. AP 1964: *Gnomon* 36 (1964): 806-808 Reinmuth. *AAHG* 17 (1964): 103 Fetz.

782. *Faber, M.* "Zum Fuenfkampf der Griechen." *Philologus* 50 (1891): 469-498.

783. *Fedde, F. Der Fuenfkampf der Hellenen.* Progr. Breslau, 1888.

784. *Fedde, F. Ueber den Fuenfkampf der Hellenen.* Leipzig, 1889.

785. *Gardiner, E. N.* "The Method of Deciding the Pentathlon." *JHS* 23 (1903): 54-70.

786. *Gardner, P.* "The Pentathlon of the Greeks." *JHS* 1 (1880): 210-223.

787. *Gruetzner, P.* "Physiologische-turnerische Betrachtungen ueber den Fuenfkampf der Griechen." *DT-Z* 51 (1906): 2-6, 17-21.

788. *Haggenmueller, H. Die Aufeinanderfolge der Kaempfe im Pentathlon.* Munich, 1892.

789. *Harris, H. A.* "The Method of Deciding Victory in the Pentathlon." *G&R* 19 (1972): 60-64.

790. *Hemelrijk, J. M.* "Het Pentathlon." *Hermeneus* 37 (1966): 116-126.

791. *Henrich, K. E. Ueber das Pentathlon der Griechen.* Diss.: Erlangen, 1892.

792. *Holwerda, A. E. J.* "Zum Pentathlon." *Arch. Zeitung.* 39 (1881): 205-216.

793. *Juethner, J. Die athletischen Leibesuebungen II.* See no. 658.

794. *Juethner, J. "Pentathlon." RE* 19, 1. Stuttgart, 1937: coll. 524-528.

795. *Legrand, Ph. E. "Quinquertium." D.-S.* 4, 1. Paris, 1907: 804-807.

796. *Maróti, E.* "Az antike pentathlon problémajához." ("On the Problem of the Ancient Pentathlon.") *Antik Tanulmányok* 1965, 2: 279-282.

797. *Marquardt, H. Zum Pentathlon der Hellenen.* Progr. Guestrow, 1886.

798. *Merkelbach, R.* "Nochmals Nikoladas aus Korinth. (Anth. Pal. XIII 19)." *ZPE* 14 (1974): 184.

799. ***Merkelbach, R.*** "Der Sieg im Pentathlon." *ZPE* 11 (1973): 261-269.

800. ***Mie, F.*** "Zum Fuenfkampf der Griechen." *JCPh* 147 (1893): 785ff.

801. ***Miller, S. G.*** "The Pentathlon for Boys at Nemea." *CSCA* 8 (1975): 199ff.

802. ***Moretti, L.*** "Un regolamento rodio per la gara del pentatlo." *RFIC* N. S. 34 (1956): 55-60.

803. ***Myers, E.*** "The Pentathlon." *JHS* 2 (1881): 217-221.

804. ***Philipp, G. F.*** *De pentathlo sive quinquertio commentatio.* Phil. Diss.: Berlin, 1827.

805. ***Pihkala, L.*** and ***Gardiner, E. N.*** "The System of the Pentathlon." *JHS* 45 (1925): 132-134.

806. ***Pinder, E.*** *Ueber den Fuenfkampf der Hellenen.* Berlin, 1867.

807. ***Reinmuth, O. W.*** *"Pentathlon." KP* 4 (1972): 618.

808. ***Scherling, K.*** "Polydamas." *RE* 21, 2. Stuttgart, 1952: col. 1601, nr. 4.

809. ***Szafka, M.*** "A *Pentathlon*-ról." ("About the Pentathlon.") *Tornaügy* 4 (1886-7): 14-16.

810. ***Szafka, M.*** "A Pentathlon felújítása." ("The Revival of the Pentathlon.") *Tornaügy* 4 (1886-7): 62-64.

G. Wrestling

811. ***Altrock, H.*** *Ringen und Schwerathletik.* Berlin, 1924. (Handbuch der Leibesuebungen 4).

812. ***Becatti, G.*** "Un gruppo ostiense di lottatori." *ASAA* N. S. 8-10 (1946-1948): 199-211.

813. ***Bulard, M.*** *"Akrokheirismós." REA* 26 (1924): 193-215.

814. ***Cazzaniga, I.*** "Osservazioni critiche intorno ai P. Oxy. 466e. P. Oxy. 2221, 1, 26, I: Frammento di manuale di lot ta del 2 sec. d. C. P. oxy. 466. *Athenaeum* 42 (1964) (Mélanges Malcovati): 373-380.

815. ***Dunst, G.*** "Die Inschrift des Periodoniken Leon." *ZPE* 3 (1968): 138-148 (144).

816. ***Ebert, J.*** *"Leosébes." ZPE* 13 (1974): 255-256.

817. ***Gardiner, E. N.*** "Wrestling I." *JHS* 25 (1905): 14-31.

818. ***Gardiner, E. N.*** "Wrestling II." *JHS* 25 (1905): 263-293.

819. ***Gardiner, E. N.*** "The Pankration and Wrestling III." See no. 871.

820. ***Goehler, J.*** "Milon von Kroton." *Die Leibeserzeihung* 4 (1955): 65-68, 87-90.

821. ***Juethner, J.*** *"Kéroma." RE* 11, 1. Stuttgart, 1921: coll. 326-328.

822. *Juethner, J.* "*Kheironomía.*" *RE* 3, 2. Stuttgart, 1899: coll. 2224-2225.

823. *Juethner, J.* "*Pale.*" *RE* 18, 3. Stuttgart, 1949: coll. 82-89.

824. *Juethner, J.* "*Skámma.*" Se no. 709.

825. *Keune, J. B.* "Straton." *RE* 4 A, 1. Stuttgart, 1931: 317-318, nr. 22.

826. *Maróti, E.* "W. Rudolph könyve az ókori olimpiák küzdösport versenyszámairól." ("W. Rudolph's Book about Combat Sports in the Ancient Olympic Games.") *Testneveléstudomány* 4 (1968): 60-61, 70. Review of no. 424.

827. *Mellor, R.* "The Athletic Leon Once Again." *ZPE* 12 (1973): 259-261. See no. 815.

828. *Merkelbach, R.* "Bacchylides auf einen Sieger in den *EMEPASIA* zu Lousoi." *ZPE* 11 (1973): 256-260.

829. *Piernavieja del Pozo, M.* "La lucha en la antigüedad." *Deporte 2000* 5 (1973) nr. 50 Marzo (with 16 illustrations).

829a. *Poliakoff, M., Studies in the Terminology of the Greek Combat Sports.* (Königstein/Ts., 1982).

830. *Reinmuth, O. W.* "Milon." *KP* 3 (1969): 1303-1304, nr. 2.

831. *Reinmuth, O. W.* "Ringkampf." *KP* 4 (1972): 1436-1437.

832. *Reisch, E.* "*Akrokheirismós.*" *RE* 1, 1. Stuttgart, 1893: coll. 1197-1198.

833. *Ridder, A. de.* "*Lucta.*" *D.-S.* 3, 2. Paris, 1904: 1340-1347.

834. *Robert, L.* "Lutteurs de Magnésie-du-Sipyle." *RPh* 1930: 42-44 (=*OMS* 11: 1142-1144.)

835. *Rudolph, W. Olympischer Kampfsport in der Antike.* See no. 424.

836. *Rudolph, W.* "Die Schwerathletik in den antiken olympischen Spielen und die Zuordnung kunstlerischer Denkmaeler zu den einzelnem Disziplinem." *Neue Beitr. zur Gesch. der Alten Welt I:* 265-273.

837. *Swoboda, H.* "Kapros 3." *RE* 10, 2. Stuttgart, 1919: coll. 1921-1922.

H. Boxing

838. *Angiolillo, Marialuisa.* "Il pugilatore della Banca del Lavoro di Roma." *Archeologia Classica* 1 (1949): 123-129.

839. *Borthwick, E. K.* "A Note on Boxing-gloves." *CR* 14 (1964): 142.

840. *Ebert, J.* "Das Epigramm fuer Hagesistratos von Rhodos." *Philologus* 3 (1967): 300-304.

841. *Frost, K. T.* "Greek Boxing." *JHS* 26 (1906): 213-225.

842. ***Hagopian, D.*** *"Pollux' Faustkampf mit Amykos. Theokrits Darstellung von demselben, verglichen mit derjenigen des Apollonius Rhodius.* Vienna: Braumueller, 1955.
Review: AP 1960: *RBPh* 38 (1960): 207 Lacroix.

843. ***Juethner, J.*** *"Caestus."* *RE* 3, 1. Stuttgart, 1897: coll. 1319-1321.

844. ***Juethner, J.*** *"Éphedros."* *RE* 5, 2. Stuttgart, 1905: coll. 2747-2748.

845. ***Juethner, J.*** and ***Mehl, E.*** *"Pygme (pugilatus)."* *RE Suppl.* 9 (1962): 1306-1352.

846. ***Kiechle, Fr.*** "Diagoras." *KP* 1 (1964): 1507, nr. 2.

847. ***Kirchner, J.*** "Diagoras." *RE* 5, 1. Stuttgart, 1913: 309-310, nr. 1.

848. ***Kirchner, J.*** "Glaukos." *RE* 7, 1. Stuttgart, 1910: 1417, nr. 33.

849. ***Maróti, E.*** "W. Rudolph könyve." See no. 826.

850. ***Mendner, S.*** "Boxhandschuhe im Altertum." *Gymnasium* 60 (1953): 20-26.

851. ***Merkelbach, R.*** "Ein agonistisches Fragment aus Side." *ZPE* 15 (1974): 227.

852. ***Merkelbach, R.*** "Herakles und der Pankratiast." *ZPE* 6 (1970): 57f.

853. ***Mohler, S. L.*** *The Cestus.* Diss.: University of Pennsylvania, Philadelphia, 1926.

854. ***Popp, H.*** "Antikes Boxen." *Oestergaards Monatshefte* 9 (1935): 137-142.

855. ***Popp, H.*** "Antikes Boxen." *Welt & Wissen* 24 (1935): 283-288.

856. ***Previale, L.*** "Il pugilato nelle letterature classiche." *MC* 1935: 90-110.

857. ***Reinmuth, O. W.*** "Boxen." *KP* 1 (1964): 938.

858. ***Reinmuth, O. W.*** *"Caestus."* *KP* 1 (1964): 1009-1010.

859. ***Reinmuth, O. W.*** *"Pygmé."* *KP* 4 (1972): 1246-1248.

860. ***Ridder, A. de.*** *"Pugilatus."* *D.-S.* 4, 1. Paris, 1907: 754-761.

861. ***Robert, L.*** "Photion de Laodicée, pugiliste." *RPH* 1930: 38-41 (=*OMS* 11: 1138-1141.)

862. ***Rudolph, W.*** *Olympischer Kampfsport in der Antike.* See no. 424.

863. ***Rudolph, W.*** "Sportverletzungen und Sportschaeden in der Antike." *Altertum* 22 (1976): 21-26.

864. ***Rudolph, W.*** "Die Schwerathletik in den antiken olympischen Spielen." See no. 836.

865. *Stegen, G.* "Un match de pugilat vu par Virgile (Énéide 5, 362-472)." *Vergiliana. Recherches sur Virgile.* publ. par Bardon, H. & Verdière, R. Roma aeterna 3. Leiden: Brill, 1971: 344-357.

866. *Thuillier, J. P.* "Le pugilat en Étrurie." *AEHE* 4e Sect. (1972-1973): 841-843.

867. *Wernicke, K.* "Amykos 2." *RE* 1, 2. Stuttgart, 1894: coll. 2000-2001.

868. *Zsingor, M.* "A régiek ökölvívása." ("Boxing of the Ancients.") *Tornaügy* 11 (1893-94): 58-63 (Depping után Zs.)

869. *Zwicker, J.* "Praxidamas." *RE* 22, 2. Stuttgart, 1954: col. 1751, nr. 1.

I. Pankration

870. *Frisch, P.* "Der Pankratiast Pergamos." *ZPE* 15 (1974): 98.

871. *Gardiner, E. N.* "The Pankration and Wrestling III." *JHS* 26 (1906): 4-22.

872. *Geisau, H. v.* "Polydamas." *KP* 4 (1972): 392-393, nr. 2.

873. *Juethner, J.* "Pankration." *RE* 18, 3. Stuttgart, 1949: coll. 619-625.

874. *Kiechle, Fr.* "Dorieus." *KP* 2 (1967): 1143, nr. 2.

875. *Kierdorf, W.* "Lygdamis." *KP* 3 (1969): 802-804, nr. 4.

876. *Maróti, E.* "W. Rudolph könyve." See no. 826.

877. *Merkelbach, R.* "Nachmals zum Dekret fuer den Pankratisten Kallikrates." *ZPE* 13 (1974): 276.

878. *Merkelbach, R.* "*Pankrátion.*" *ZPE* 5 (1970): 30-31.

879. *Merkelbach, R.* "Der unentschiedene Kampf des Pankratiasten Ti. Claudius Rufus in Olympia." *ZPE* 15 (1974): 99-104.

880. *Obst.* "Lygdamis." *RE* 13, 2. Stuttgart, 1927: col. 2217, nr. 5.

881. *Reinmuth, O.W.* "Pankration." *KP* 4 (1972): 460.

882. *Robert, L.* "M. Aurelius Demostratos Damas, pancratiaste." *RPh* 1930: 44-49 (=*OMS* 11: 1144-1149).

883. *Rudolph, W.* *Olympischer Kampfsport in der Antike.* See no. 424.

884. *Rudolph, W.* "Die Schwerathletik in den antiken olympischen Spielen." See no. 836.

J. Greek Equestrian Events

885. *Anderson, J. K.* *Ancient Greek Horsemanship.* With a Transl. of Xenophon's *Peri hippikes.* Berkeley: Univ. of Calif. Pr., 1961.

Reviews: AP 1965: *AIHS* 17 (1964): 188-189 Godard. AP 1964: *CPh* 59 (1964): 217-218 Moritz. *REG* 77 (1964): 575-576 Chamoux. AP 1963: *JHS* 83 (1963): 206 Benton. *Archaeology* 16 (1963): 65 Markman. AP 1962: *CR* 12 (1962): 317 Farrington. *CJ* 58 (1962): 36 Jacks. *CW* 55 (1962): 199 Milhauser. *REA* 64 (1962): 462-463 Delebecque. *AHR* 67 (1961-1962): 463 Rexine. *ArchClass* 13 (1961): 245-246 Bonacasa.

886. ***Anderson, J. K.*** "Homeric, British, and Cyrenaic Chariots." *AJA* 2nd Series, 76 (1972): 17-22.

887. ***Brauer, G. C.*** "The Kalpe. An Agonistic Reference on Several Greek Coins?" *San* 6 (1974/75): 6f.

888. ***Delebecque, E.*** *Le cheval dans l'Iliade.* See no. 208.

889. ***Gebhard, V.*** "Taraxippos." *RE* 4 A, 2. Stuttgart, 1932: coll. 2288-2289.

890. ***Geisau, H. v.*** "Taraxippos." *KP* 5 (1975): 517.

891. ***Greenhalgh, P. A. L.*** *Early Greek Warfare. Horsemen and Chariots in the Homeric and Archaic Ages.* Cambridge University Press, 1973.

892. ***Harris, H. A.*** "Rubrification in Antiquity." *G&R* 21 (1974): 32-36.

893. ***Harris, H. A.*** "The Starting-gate for Chariots. A Post-Script." *G&R* 16 (1969): 172-173.

894. ***Harris, H. A.*** "The Starting-gate for Chariots at Olympia." *G&R* 15 (1968): 113-126.

895. ***Harris, H. A.*** Chapters VII, VIII and IX in *Sport in Greece and Rome.* See no. 51.

896. ***Hermann, G.*** *De hippodromo olympiaco.* Phil. Diss: Leipzig, 1839.

897. ***Hill, D. K.*** "Chariots of Early Greece." *Hesperia* 43, No. 4 (1974): 441-446.

898. ***Hug, A.*** *"Sunorís."* *RE* 4 A, 2. Stuttgart, 1932: coll. 1450-1452.

899. ***Jankovich, M.*** *They Rode into Europe. The Fruitful Exchange in the Arts of Horsemanship between East and West.* London: Harrap, 1971.

Review: AP 1971: *Antiquity* 45 (1971): 230-231 Piggott.

900. ***Kirchner, J.*** "Belistiche." *RE* 3, 1. Stuttgart, 1897: col. 240.

901. ***Lafaye, G.*** *"Equitatio." D.-S.* 2, 1. Paris, 1892: 746-752.

902. ***Lehndorff, G.*** *Hippodromos. Einiges ueber Pferde und Rennen im griechischen Altertum.* Berlin, 1876.

903. ***Lippold, G.*** "Kleoitas." *RE* 11, 1. Stuttgart, 1921: coll. 675-676.

904. ***Martin, A.*** *"Equites." D.-S.* 2, 1. Paris, 1892: 752-771.

905. ***Martin, A.*** *"Hippodromos." D.-S.* 3, 1. Paris, 1896: 193-210.

906. ***Merklin, E. v.*** *Der Rennwagen in Griechenland.* Phil. Diss.: Leipzig, 1909.

907. ***Morissey, E. J.*** "Victors in the Prytaneion Decree. (IG I^2 77)." *GRBS* 19 (1978): 121-125.

908. ***Nuoffer, O.*** *Der Rennwagen im Altertum.* Diss.: Leipzig: Hallberg und Buechting, 1904.

909. ***Picard, Ch.*** "Le sculpteur Cleoitas, fils d'Aristoclès, et les automates de l'Aphésis à l'Hippodrome d'Olympie." *RA* 1963: 107-108.

910. ***Picard, Ch.*** "Sur un motif du char archaïque en course." *RA* 6e Ser. 43 (1954): 220-224.

911. ***Poole, L. & G.*** "Chariot Racing in Ancient Greece." *Greek Heritage* 1, No. 2 (1964): 4-10.

912. ***Popplow, U.*** "Totenkult und Wagenrennen in Alt-Mykene." See no. 196.

913. ***Preedy, J. B. K.*** "The Chariot Group of the Maussoleum." See no. 1374.

914. ***Reinmuth, O. W.*** *"Auriga." KP* 1 (1964): 772.

915. ***Reisch, E.*** *"Anabátes." RE* 1, 2. Stuttgart, 1894: coll. 2014-2015.

916. ***Reisch, E.*** *"Anthippasía." RE* 1, 2. Stuttgart, 1894: coll. 2378-2379.

917. ***Reisch, E.*** *"Apéne." RE* 1, 2. Stuttgart, 1894: coll. 2695-2696.

918. ***Reisch, E.*** *"Aphesis." RE* 1, 2. Stuttgart, 1894: coll. 2715-2717.

919. ***Reisch, E.*** *"Aphippodromás." RE* 1, 2. Stuttgart, 1894: col. 2721.

920. ***Reisch, E.*** *"Aphippolampás." RE* 1, 2. Stuttgart, 1894: col. 2721.

921. ***Reisch, E.*** *"Aphippotoxótai." RE* 1, 2. Stuttgart, 1894: coll. 2721-2722.

922. ***Reisch, E.*** *"Apobátes." RE* 1, 2. Stuttgart, 1894: coll. 2814-2817.

923. ***Schneider, K.*** *"Hippodromos 2." RE* 8, 2. Stuttgart, 1913: coll. 1735-1745.

924. ***Schneider, K.*** *"Kálpes drómos." RE* 10, 2. Stuttgart, 1919: coll. 1760-1761.

925. ***Schneider, K.*** "Quadriga." *RE* 24, 1. 1963: coll. 681-686.

926. ***Turner, E. G.*** "The Charioteer from Antinoe." *JHS* 93 (1973): 192-95.

927. ***Vanderpool, E.*** "Victories in the Anthippasia." *Hesperia* 43, No. 3 (1974): 311-313. (Contests among cavalry units.)

928. ***Van Merklin, E.*** "Chariots on Geometric Vases." *AJA* 20, No. 3 (1916).

929. ***Vigneron, P.*** *Le cheval dans l'antiquité gréco-romaine (des guerres médiques aux grandes invasions). Contribution à l'histoire des techniques.* Annales de l'Est Nancy Fac. des lettres, 1968.

Reviews: AP 1969: *REL* 47 (1969): 667-668 Sauvage. *REG* 82 (1969): 606-608 Delebecque.

930. ***Widdra, K. O.*** *Xenophons "Reitkunst".* Phil. Diss.: Marburg, 1959.

931. ***Wiesner, J.*** "Fahren und Reiten." *Archaeologia Homerica. Die Denkmaeler und das fruehgriechische Epos.* Auftr. des Dt. Archaeol. Inst. Matz, F. and Buccholz, H. G., eds. Goettingen: Vanderhoeck & Ruprecht, 1968.

K. Greek Aquatic Sports and Games

932. ***Auriga, M.*** "Gedanken ueber das Fehlen des Schwimmwettkampfes bei den allhellenischen Spielen." *LKE* 57 (1938): 206-211.

933. ***Auriga, M.*** "Bei der Ur-Olympischen Spielen finden wir nichts von einem Schwimmwettkampf. Was moegen die Gruende dafuer gewesen sein?" *Die Leibeserziehung* 1956: 370-374.

934. ***Couch, H. N.*** "Swimming among the Greeks and Barbarians." *CJ* 29 (1934): 609-612.

935. ***Gardner, P.*** "Boat-races among the Greeks." *JHS* 2 (1881): 90-97.

936. ***Gardner, P.*** "Boat-races at Athens." See no. 566.

937. ***Gardner, P.*** "A Stele Commemorating a Victory in a Boat Race." *JHS* 11 (1890): 146-150.

938. ***Geiss, A.*** "Warum die Hellenen das Schwimmen nicht in ihre Agonistik aufgenommen haben?" *HfL* 9 (1929): 94-95.

939. ***Ginouves, R.*** *Balaneutiké. Recherches sur le bain dans l'antiquité grecque.* Paris, 1962.

940. ***Holloway, R. R.*** "High Flying at Paestum. A Reply." *AJA* 81 (1977): 554-555. Reply to W. J. Slater. See no. 954.

941. ***McGrail, S.*** and ***Farrell, A.*** "Rowing. Aspects of the Ethnographic and Iconographic Evidence." *IJNA* 8 (1979): 155-166.

942. ***Mehl, E.*** *Antike Schwimmkunst.* Munich, 1927.

943. ***Mehl, E.*** *Antike Schwimmkunst und (antikes) Schwimmen.* Wien: Habil-Schrift, 1941.

944. ***Mehl, E.*** "Antikes Brust-und Beinschlagswimmen." *Die Leibesuebungen* 2 (1926): 41ff.

945. ***Mehl, E.*** "Schwimmen." *RE Suppl.* 5 (1931): 847-864.

946. ***Mehl, E.*** "Ueber antike Schwimm-und Wasserspringstile." *Die Leibesuebungen* 1 (1925): 377ff.

947. ***Mehl, E.*** "Warum bevorzugen die antiken Kulturvoelker das Schlagschwimmen, die Deutschen dagegen das Stosschwimmen?" *Olymp. Rdsch.* 8 (1940): 24-26.

948. ***Morrison, J. S.*** and ***Williams, R. T.*** *Greek Oared Ships. 900-322 B. C.* Cambridge Univ. Press, 1968.

Reviews: AP 1968: *CW* 62 (1968): 51 Casson. *Hermathena* 107 (1968): 77 Hinds. *LEC* 36 (1968): 295 Wankenne. AP 1969: *CR* 19 (1969): 227-229 Cook. *CPh* 64 (1969): 180-182 Anderson *G&R* 15 (1969): 111 Sewter. *CJ* 64 (1969): 284-287 Mackendrick.

949. ***Pottier, E.*** *"Urinator." D.-S.* 5. Paris, 1914: 604.

950. ***Reuel, F.*** "Warum die alten Griechen kein Wettschwimmen abzuhalten pflegten." *Die Leibesuebungen* 6 (1930): 31f.

951. ***Sakellarios, P. G.*** "He kolumbetikè kaì he dutikè tõn arkhaîon Hellénon." *PAA* 33 (1958): 379-397.

952. ***Sanders, H. A.*** "Swimming among the Greeks and Romans." *CJ* 20 (1924): 566-568.

953. ***Schuetze, K.*** "Warum kannten die Griechen keine Schwimmwettkampfe?" *Hermes* 73 (1938): 355-357.

954. ***Slater, W. J.*** "High Flying at Paestum." *AJA* 80 (1976): 423-425.

955. ***Slater, W. J.*** "High Flying at Paestum. Further Comments." *AJA* 81 (1977); 555-557. Reply to R. R. Holloway, this section.

956. ***Tilley, A. F.*** "An Experiment under Oars." *Antiquity* 45 (1971): pl. 10-11.

957. ***Tilley, A. F.*** and ***Fenwick, V. H.*** "Rowing in the Mediterranean. A New Aspect." *Mariner's Mirror* 59 (London Soc. for Nautical Research) (1973): 96-100.

958. ***Vries, K. de.*** "Diving into the Mediterranean." *Expedition* 21, 1 (1978): 4-8.

959. ***Wágner, J.*** "Uszósport az ókorban." ("Swimming in Antiquity.") *Testnevelés* 6 (1933): 131-139, 245-257.

L. Greek Ball Games

960. ***Delande, J.*** "Le football à travers les âges." *LEC* 1940: 409-414.

961. ***Goepel, M.*** *Beitraege zur Geschichte des Ballspiels.* Progr. Eberswalde, 1909.

962. ***Gruendel, L.*** "Griechische Ballspiele." *AA* (1925): 80-95.

963. ***Hessel, E.*** "Das Spiel Phaininda-Harpastum." *Gymnasium* 67 (1960): 226.
964. ***Heubaum, R.*** "Ueber Galens "Spiel mit dem kleinen" Ball" und seine groesste Streitschrift gegen die Athleten." *LKE* 58 (1939): 198-202.
965. ***Hirn, A.*** "Spielten bei den Griechen Fussball?" *LKE* 54 (1935): 479-482.
966. ***Kroll, W.*** *"Phenínda." RE* 19, 2. Stuttgart, 1938: col. 1980.
967. ***Lafaye, G.*** *"Pila." D.-S.* 4, 1. Paris, 1907: 475-478.
968. ***Mau,*** "Ballspiel." *RE* 2, 2. Stuttgart, 1869: coll. 2832-2834.
969. ***Mau,*** *"Epískyros." RE* 6, 1. Stuttgart, 1907: coll. 199-200.
970. ***Mau,*** *"Expulsim." RE* 6, 2. Stuttgart, 1909: coll. 1694-1695.
971. ***Mau,*** *"Follis 2." RE* 6, 2. Stuttgart, 1909: col. 2829.
972. ***Mendner, S.*** *Das Ballspiel im Leben der Voelker.* Muenster: Aschendorff, 1956.
Review: AP 1960: *CPh* 55 (1960): 210-211 Pickel.
973. ***Mendner, S.*** "Gesellschaftsspiele." (Abschnitt Ballspiele.) *RLAC* 10 (1978) Lief. 78: 847-895.
974. ***Mendner, S.*** "Das Spiel Phaininda-Harpastum." *Gymnasium* 66 (1959): 517-524.
975. ***Merker, J.*** "Der griechische Arzt Galen und das Ballspiel." *LKE* 55 (1936): 104.
976. ***Mitchell, L. B.*** "Ancient Ball Games." *CJ* 34 (1938): 103.
977. ***Nickel, D.*** "Ein Ballspiel im Urteil des Arztes. Bemerkungen zu Galens Schrift, Ueber die Uebung mit dem kleinen Ball." *NTM* 13 (1976): 77-81.
978. ***Oikonomos, G.*** *"Keretízontes." Arkh. Deltíon* 6 (1920-1921): 56-59.
979. ***Radke, G.*** *"Trigon." RE* 7 A, 1. Stuttgart, 1939: col. 139.
980. ***Saglio, E.*** *"Corycus." D.-S.* 1, 2. Paris, 1887: 1541.
981. ***Schnieder, K.*** *"Harpastum." RE* 7. Stuttgart, 1912: coll. 2405-2407.
982. ***Schneider, K.*** *"Sphairistérion." RE* 3 A, 2. Stuttgart, 1929: coll. 1680-1682.
983. ***Schneider, K.*** *"Sphairomakhía." RE* 3 A, 2. Stuttgart, 1929: col. 1682.
984. ***Schuppe, E.*** *"Paganica." RE* 18, 2. Stuttgart, 1942: col. 2295.
985. ***Takács, M.*** "Római labajátékok." ("Roman Ball Games.") *Herkules* 10 (1893): 196.
986. ***Tod, M. N.*** "Teams of Ball-Players at Sparta." *ABSA* 10 (1903-1904): 63-77.
987. ***Tod, M. N.*** "Three New *SPHRAIREIS*-Inscriptions." *ABSA* 13 (1906-1907): 212-218.

988. ***Wagner, E.*** "Hockeyspiel im Altertum." *Philologus* 103 (1959): 137-140.

989. ***Wagner, E.*** "Kritische Bemerkungen zum Harpastum-Spiel." *Gymnasium* 70 (1963): 356-366.

990. ***Weyens, P.*** "Het balspel in de klassieke oudheid." Thèse de licence: Univ. de Louvain; cf. *RBPh* 1942: 538.

991. ***Woodward, A. M.*** "Some Notes on the Spartan *Sphaireis.*" *ABSA* 46 (1951): 191-199.

992. ***Young, N.*** "Did the Greeks and Romans Play Football?" *Research Quarterly* 15 (1944): 310-316.

M. Miscellaneous Greek Events

993. ***Bérard, J.*** "Le concours de l'arc dans l'Odyssée." *REG* 68 (1955): 1-11.

994. ***Brackova, M.*** "Les jouets d'enfants dans l'antiquité." (in Bulgarian) *Arch (Sofia)* 1960, 1: 57-59.

995. ***Brain, P.*** and ***Skinner, D. D.*** "Odysseus and the Axes: Homeric Ballistics Reconstructed." *G&R* 25 (1978): 55ff.

996. ***Burkert, W.*** "Von Amenophis II. zur Bogenprobe des Odysseus." *GB* 1 (1973): 69-78.

997. ***Butler, A. J.*** *Sport in Classic Times.* London: Benn, and New York: Dutton, 1930, reprinted Los Altos, Calif.: W. Kaufmann, 1975.
Review: AP 1932: *CW* 25 (1931): 44 Fraser.

998. ***Gross, W. H.*** *"Toxon." KP* 5 (1975): 903.

999. ***Herter, H.*** "Das Leben ein Kinderspiel." *BJ* 161 (1961): 73-84.

1000. ***Hett, W. S.*** "The Games of the Greek Boy." *G&R* 1 (1931): 24-29.

1001. ***Hull, D. B.*** *Hounds and Hunting in Ancient Greece.* Chicago: Univ. of Chicago Pr., 1964.
Review: *AP* 1964: *Athene (Chicago)* 25, 3 (1964): 28.

1002. ***Hull, D. B.*** "Hunting in Ancient Hellas." *Greek Heritage* 1, No. 1 (1963): 32-36.

1003. ***Juethner, J.*** *"Hoplites 3." RE* 8, 2. Stuttgart, 1913: coll. 2297-2298.

1004. ***Juethner, J.*** *"Hoplomachie." RE* 8, 2. Stuttgart, 1913: coll. 2298-2299.

1005. ***Juethner, J.*** *"Kybistetér." RE* 11, 2. Stuttgart, 1922: coll. 2299-2230.

1006. ***Juethner, J.*** *"Korykomakhía." RE* 11, 2. Stuttgart, 1922: coll. 1450-1451.

1007. ***Juethner, J.*** *"Kórykos 5." RE* 11, 2. Stuttgart, 1922: coll. 1452-1453.

1008. ***Juethner, J.*** *"Euandrías agón."* See no. 569.

1009. ***Lambert, F.*** *"Toxótai."* *RE* 6 A, 2. Stuttgart, 1937: coll. 1853-1855.

1010. ***Lambin, G.*** "Les formules de jeux d'enfants dans la Grèce antique." *REG* 88 (1975): 168-177.

1011. ***Lefebvre-Verreydt, B.*** "Twee kinderspelen uit de oudheid." *Kleio* 5 (1975): 83-89.

1012. ***McCartney, E. S.*** "Marvelous Feats of Archery." *CJ* 35 (1940): 537-541.

1013. ***McLeod, W. E.*** "Archery in Ancient Greece." *Greek Heritage* 1, No. 3 (1964).

1014. ***McLeod, W. E.*** "The Range of the Ancient Bow." *Phoenix* 19 (1965): 1-14.

1015. ***Mehl, E.*** "Turnkunst." *RE* 7 A, 2. Stuttgart, 1948: coll. 2513-2556.

1016. ***Merkelbach, R.*** "Ephesische Parerga (12). Eine *Tabula lusoria* fuer den *ludus latrunculorum.*" *ZPE* 28 (1978): 48-50.

1017. ***Miltner, Helene.*** *"Tóxon."* *RE* 6, 2. Stuttgart, 1937: coll. 1847-1853.

1018. ***Mingazzini, P.*** "Tre giochi infantili antichi." *RPAA* 32 (1959-1960): 81-92.

1019. ***Mommsen, H.*** "Achill und Aias pflichtsvergessen?" *Tainia. Roland Hampe zur 70. Geburtstag am 2. Dezember dargebracht.* Cahn, H. A. and Simon, E., eds. Vol. I: text; Vol. II: plates. Mainz: von Zabern, 1980: 138-152.

1020. ***Orth, E.*** "Jagd." *RE* 9, 1. Stuttgart, 1914: coll. 558-604.

1021. ***Perdrizet, P. F.*** "The Game of Morra." *JHS* 18 (1898): 129-132.

1022. ***Reisch, E.*** *"Agon(es)."* *RE* 1. Stuttgart, 1894: 838-840.

1023. ***Ridgeway, W.*** "The Game of Polis and Plato's Republic 422 E." *JHS* 16 (1896): 288-290.

1024. ***Rohles, G.*** *Antikes Knoechelspiel im einstigen Grossgriechenland. Eine vergleichende historisch-linguistische Studie.* Tuebingen: Niemeyer, 1963.

Reviews: AP 1965: *Zs. fuer Volkskunde* (Stuttgart) 61 (1965): 306-307 Werner. AP 1964: *RPh* 38 (1964): 332 Ernout. *AAHG* 16 (1963): 229 Thummer.

1025. ***Saglio, E.*** *"Arcus."* *D.-S.* 1, 1. Paris, 1877: 388-391.

1026. ***Saglio, E.*** *"Hoplomachia."* *D.-S.* 3, 1. Paris, 1899: 248-249.

1027. ***Schaumberg, A.*** *Bogen und Bogenschiessen bei den Griechen.* Nuremburg, 1910.

1028. ***Schmidt, Eva.*** *Spielzeug und Spiele der Kinder im klassischen Altertum. Mit Beispielen aus den Bestaenden des Deutschen Spielzeugmuseums Sonneberg.* Suedthuer. Forsch. 7, 71. Meiningen Staatl. Mus., 1971.

Review: AP 1978: *Gnomon* 50 (1978); 675-678 Herter.

1029. ***Schneider, K.*** *"Korýkeion 2."* *RE* 11, 2. Stuttgart, 1922: col. 1448.

1030. ***Stern, E. von.*** "Der Pfeilschuss des Olbiopoliten Anaxagoras." *JOeAI* 4 (1901) Beibl.: coll. 57-60.

1031. ***Tilander, G.*** *Cynegetica, 8: Nouveaux mélanges d'etymologie cynégétique.* Stockholm: Almquist & Wiksell, 1961.

Review: AP 1964: *Romania* 85 (1964): 142-144.

1032. ***Zazoff, P.*** "Ephedrismos. Ein altgriechisches Spiel." *A&A* 11 (1962): 35-42.

VII

ROMAN ATHLETICS

General

1033. ***Auguet, R.*** *Cruauté et civilisation. Les jeux romains.* Paris: Flammarion, 1970.

Reviews: AP 1972: *RS* 92 (1971): 146. AP 1971: *RACF* 9 (1970): 320.

1034. ***Auguet, R.*** *Cruelty and Civilization. The Roman Games.* London: Allen & Unwin, 1972.

Reviews: AP 1975: *CR* 25 (1975): 156-157 Ogilvie. *G&R* 20 (1973): 209-210 Walcot. *TLS* 71 (1972): 1564.

1035. ***Balil, A.*** "Notas de lectura (l'une sur les jeux du cirque)." *Durius* 1 (1973): 371-377.

1036. ***Balsdon, J. P. V. D.*** "Panem et circenses." *Hommages à Marcel Renard.* Bibauw, J., ed. Coll. Latomus 101, 102, & 103: Bruxelles: 60 rue Colonel Chaltin, 1969. Vol. 2: 57-60.

1037. ***Baracconi, C.*** *Spettacoli nell'antica Roma.* Roma: Edizioni del Gattopardo, 1972.

1038. ***Benario, H. W.,*** "Sport at Rome." *AncW* 7 (1983) 39-43.

1039. ***Booth, A. D.*** "Roman Attitudes to Physical Education." *EMC* 19 (1975): 27-34.

1040. ***Buchanan, D.*** *Roman Sport and Entertainment.* Aspects of Greek and Roman Life. London: Longman, 1976.

1041. ***Buechner, J.*** *De spectaculis.* Diss.: Wuerzburg, 1935.

1042. ***Colini, A. M.*** and ***Cozza, L.*** *Ludus Magnus.* Rome: Monte dei paschi di Siena, 1962.

1043. ***Edelstein, L.*** "Antike diaetetik." See no. 239.

1044. ***Friedlander, L.*** *Roman Life and Manners under the Early Empire.* 4 vols. London: G. Routledge, and New York: E. P. Dutton, 1908-13, English Translation of the 7th ed. of *Darstellungen aus der Sittengeschichte Roms.*

1045. ***Gassowska, B.*** *Jouets grecs et romains.* See no. 42.

1046. ***Gedda, L.*** *Lo Sport.* See no. 43.

1047. ***Gostkowski, R.*** "Le sport dans l'antiquité." See no. 48.

1048. ***Grasberger, L.*** *Erziehung und Unterricht im klasischen Altertum.* See no. 49.

1049. ***Harris, H. A.*** *Sport in Greece and Rome.* See no. 51.

1050. ***Heubaum, R.*** "Das hellenische-roemische Bildungsideal und die koerperliche Erziehung." See no. 52.

1051. ***Hirn, A.*** "Die Leibesuebungen bei den Roemern." *HfL* 7 (1929).

1052. ***Huber, K.*** "Theorie der gymnischen Erziehung bei den Roemern." *Friedrich Manns Paedagogisches Magazin* 1411 (1934).

1053. ***Huizinga, J.*** *Homo Ludens,* See no. 59.

1054. *Jeux Dans l'antiquité.* See no. 64.

1055. ***Jung, A.*** *Massage und Sport im Altertum und Gegenwart.* See no. 74.

1056. ***Lennartz, K.*** *Kenntnisse und Vorstellungen von Olympia und den olympischen Spielen in der Zeit von 393-1896.* See no. 382.

1057. ***Maehl, E.*** *Gymnastik und Athletik im Denken der Roemer.* Heuremata 2. Amsterdam: Gruener, 1974.

1058. ***Marrou, H. I.*** *A History of Education in Antiquity.* See nos. 99 and 100 (English and French).

1059. ***Méautis, G.*** "Sports antiques et sports modernes." See no. 101.

1060. ***Mehl, E.*** "Altroemische Heersturnen." *Festgabe Mehl,* Anhang: 13-21. (Bundesturnzeitung Wien 1927, revis-ed.) See Jahn, no. 62.

1061. ***Paulinès, E.*** *Historía tes gymnastikes.* See no. 119.

1062. ***Piganiol, A.*** *Recherches sur les jeux romains.* Strasbourg: Librairie Istra, and New York: Columbia University Press, 1923.

1063. ***Pighi, G. B.*** *De ludis saecularibus populi Romani.* Amsterdam: Schippers, 1965. (Repr. of 1941 ed.)

1064. ***Poynton, J. B.*** "The Public Games of the Romans." *G&R* 7 (1938): 76-85.

1065. ***Renson, R.: Nayer, P. P. de;*** and **Ostin, M., eds.** *The History, the Evolution and the Diffusion of Sports.* See no. 137.

1066. ***Rudolph, W.*** "Antike Sportgeraete." See no. 145.

1067. ***Saglio, E.*** *"Certamina." D.-S.* 1, 2. Paris, 1887: 1080-1086.

1068. ***Saurbier, B.*** and ***Stahr, E.*** *Geschichte der Leibesuebungen.* See no. 149.

1069. ***Servadio, E.*** "Sport." See no. 153.

1070. ***Stiebitz, F.*** "La gymnastique et le sport dans l'antiquité." See no. 154.

1071. ***Termes, Ch. M.*** *Introduction à la civilisation romaine.* Vol. I: *Les Jeux.* Luxenbourg: Centre Alexandre-Wiltheim Sér Réflexions I, 1980.

1072. ***Ueberhorst, H.*** *Geschichte der Leibesuebungen.* See no. 162.

1073. ***Vaeterlein, J.*** *Roma ludens. Kinder und Erwachsene beim Spiel im Antiken Rom.* Heuremata 5. Amsterdam: Gruener, 1976.

Reviews: AP 1978: *Gymnasium* 85 (1978): 371-373 Wachsmuth. *EAZ* 19 (1978): 738-739 Fischer. *Gnomon* 50 (1978): 675-678 Herter. *AAHG* 31 (1978): 251 Scheer. AP 1977: *REL* 54 (1976): 490 Béranger. *MH* 34 (1977): 271 Borle. *LEC* 1977: 181-182 Zachová. *BFLM* 7 (1976-1977): 81-82 Thill.

1074. ***Vanzetti, M.*** "Iuvenes turbolenti." *Labeo* 20 (1974): 77-82.

1075. ***Vogt, M.*** *Der Antike Sport* and "Der Sport im Altertum." See nos. 167 and 168.

1076. ***Wacke, A.*** "Athleten als Darlehensnehmer nach roemischem Recht." *Gymnasium* 86 (1979): 149-164.

1077. ***Wacke, A.*** "Unfaelle bei Sport und Spiel nach roemischen und geltendem Recht." *Stadion* 3 (1977): 4-43.

1078. ***Weiler, I.*** *Der Sport bei den Voelker der alten Welt.* See no. 170.

VIII

THE ORIGINS AND DEVELOPMENT OF ROMAN ATHLETICS

A. Etruscan, Early Roman, and Republican Athletics

1079. ***Bargellini, P.*** *Die Kunst der Etrusker.* Vienna, Hamburg: Zsolnay, 1969.

1080. ***Bartocinni, R.; Lerici, C. M.*** and ***Moretti, M.*** *Tarquinia. La tomba delle olimpiadi.* Milano: Lerici, 1959.

Reviews: AP 1959: *RSC* 7 (1959): 316-318 Scamuzzi. *RA* 1 (1959): 238-240 Chevallier.

1081. ***Beazley, J. D.*** *Etruscan Vase-painting.* Oxford Monogr. on Class. Archaeol. Oxford Univ. Pr., 1947.

1082. ***Bloch, R.*** *Die Kunst der Etrusker.* Stuttgart, Berlin, Cologne, Mainz: Kohlhammer, 1966.

1083. ***Bronson, R. C.*** "Chariot Racing in Etruria." *Studi in onore di L. Banti.* Rome: L'Erma, 1965: 89-106.

1084. ***Diem, C.*** "Etruskischer Sport." *Olympische Rundschau* H. 15 (1941): 1-8. (=Olympische Flamme 2: 603-611.)

1085. ***Diem, C.*** *Das Trojanische Reiterspiel.* Berlin, 1942.

1086. ***Fowler, W. W.*** *The Roman Festivals of the Period of the Republic.* New York: Gordon Pr., 1977. reprint of 1899 edition.

1087. ***Gerhard, E.; Klugemann, A.*** and ***Koerte, G.*** *Etruskische Spiegel.* Berlin: G. Reimer, 1840-1847.

1088. ***Giglioli, G. Q.*** "L'oinochoe de Tragliatella." *SE* 3 (1929): 116-135.

1089. ***Gordziejew, W.*** *Ludi scaenici et circenses qui in rebus publicis antiquorum valuerint.* Warsaw: Univ. Pilsudski, 1936.

Reviews: AP 1940-41: *Gnomon* 1940: 94 Lesky. AP 1939: *PhW* 1939: 542-545 Eichenberg. *Eos* 1937: 376-377 Sinko. *CR* 1939: 225 Whittick. AP 1938: *REA* 1938: 77 Herrmann. *CW* 31 (1938): 155 McDaniel. *Przeglad Klasyczny* 4 (1938): 147-149 Rozenberg (Suppl. bibl.)

1090. ***Grothe, H.*** "Das Troianische Reiterspiel." *Deutschland in Geschichte und Gegenwart* Heft 3 (1975).

1091. ***Heller, J. L.*** "Labyrinth or Troy Town?" *CJ* 42 (1946): 123-139.

1092. ***Heurgon, J.*** "Die Spiele." *Die Etrusker: Kunst und Geschichte.* Munich: Hirmen, 1977: 277-309.

1093. ***Hus, A.*** "Les jeux publics et funéraires en Étrurie." *CEA* 6 (1977): 59-71.

1094. ***Johnstone, M. A.*** *The Dance in Etruria. A Comparative Study.* Florence: Olschki, 1956.
Review: AP 1956: *Zephyrus* 7 (1956): 263 Blázquez.

1095. ***Kastelic, J.*** *Situlenkunst.* Vienna: Schroll, 1964.

1096. ***Knight, W. F. J.*** "Maze Symbolism and the Trojan Game." *Antiquity* 6 (1932): 445ff.

1097. ***Mehl, E.*** "Altroemisches Heeresturnen. (1927)" *Festgabe Mehl,* 13ff. See Jahn, no. 62.

1098. ***Mehl, E.*** "Troiaespiel." *RE Suppl.* 8 (1956): 888-905.

1099. ***Moretti, M.*** and ***Matt, L. von.*** *Etruskische Malerei in Tarquinia.* Cologne: DuMont Schauberg, 1974.

1100. ***Pallotino, M.*** *Die Etrusker.* Frankfurt: Fisher, 1955. (repr. of 1942 ed.) *The Etruscans.* J. Cremona, Engl. trans. Revised edition, N. Y.: Penguin, 1978.

1101. ***Pfiffig, A. J.*** *Einfuehrung in die Etruskologie. Probleme, Methoden, Ergebnisse.* Altertumswiss. Einfuehr. in Gegenstand, Methoden & Ergebnisse ihrer Teildisziplinem & Hilfswiss. Darmstadt, Wiss. Buchges, 1972.

1102. ***Root, M. C.*** "An Etruscan Horse Race from Poggio Civitate." *AJA* 77 (April 1973): 121-137.

1103. ***Sawula, L. W.*** *Physical Activities in the Etruscan Civilization.* M. A. Thesis: Univ. of Alberta, Edmonton, 1969.

1104. ***Schmidtchen, V.*** and ***Howell, M.*** "Leibesuebungen bei den Etruskern. Ein problemorientierter Ueberblick." See Ueberhorst, *Geschichte der Leibesuebungen,* vol. 2: 168-199, no. 162.

1105. ***Schneider, K.*** *"Lusus Troiae."* *RE* 13. Stuttgart, 1927: 2056-2067.

1106. ***Strohmeyer, H.*** "Die Leibesuebungen in der Situlenkunst." *Leibeserziehung* 18 (1969): 144-151.

1107. ***Thuillier, J. P.*** "Le pugiliat en Étrurie." See no. 866.

1108. ***Weeber, K. W.*** *"Troiae lusus.* Alter und Entstehung eines Reiterspiels." *AncSoc* 5 (1974): 171-196.

1109. ***Weege, F.*** "Etruskische Graeber mit Gemaelden in Corneto," *JDAI* 31 (1916): 105-168.

B. Athletics During the Empire

1110. ***Balsdon, J. P. V. D.*** *Life and Leisure in Ancient Rome.* New York: McGraw Hill, 1969.

1111. ***Becker, W. A.*** and ***Goell, H.*** *Gallus oder roemische Szenen aus der Zeit Augustus.* Berlin, 1880[2]: 168-188. on Roman Sports.

1112. ***Beltrán Lloris, M.*** "Una celebrazión de Ludi en territorio de Gallur Zaragoza." *14 Congr. archaeologique. Cronica del XIV Congreso arqueologico nacional (Vitoria 1975).* Zaragoza: Semin. de Arqueol. de la Univ., 1977: 1061-1070.

1113. ***Bollinger, T.*** *Theatralis licentia. Die Publikumsdemonstrationen an oeffentlichen Spielen im Rom der Kaiserzeit und ihre Bedeutung im politischen Leben.* Diss.: Winterthur: Hans Schellenberg, 1969.

1114. ***Brind'Amour, P.*** "L'origine des jeux séculaires." *Aufstieg und Niedergang der roemischen Welt.* Temporini, H. and Haase, W., eds. vol. 16, 2. (1978): 1334ff.

1115. ***Cameron, A.*** *Bread and Circuses: the Emperor and the Roman People.* Inaugural lecture at King's College, London, 1974.

1116. ***Cameron, A.*** *Circus Factions. Blues and Greens at Rome and Byzantium.* Oxford: Clarendon Press, 1976.

1117. ***Cameron, A.*** "Demos and Factions." *ByzZ* 67 (1974): 74-91.

1118. ***Carcopino, J.*** *Rom. Leben und Kultur in der Kaiserzeit.* neu hrsg. von Pack, E. Stuttgart: Reclam, 1977. (repr. of 1939 ed.) *Daily Life in Ancient Rome.* H. T. Rowell, ed. E. O. Lorimer, Engl. trans. New Haven and London: Yale Univ. Press, 1940.

1119. ***Cavallars, M. A.*** "Economia e religio nei ludi secolari augustei." *RhM* 122 (1979): 49ff.

1120. ***Deininger, J.*** "Brot und Spiele." Tacitus und die Entpolitisierung der *plebs urbana.*" *Gymnasium* 86 (1979): 278-303.

1121. ***Gentili, G. V.*** "Studi e ricerche sull'anfiteatro di Siracusa." *Palladio* 23 (1973): 3-80.

1122. ***Goellmann, C.*** *Zur Beurteilung der oeffentlichen Spiele Roms bei Tacitus, Plinius dem Juengeren, Martial und Juvenal.* Diss.: Muenster, 1942.

1123. ***Habel.*** *"Ludi publici." RE Suppl.* 5 (1931): coll. 608-630.

1124. ***Harmon, D. P.*** "The Family Festivals of Rome." *Aufstieg und Niedergang der roemischen Welt.* Temporini, H. and Haase, W., eds. 16, 2 (1978): 1592ff.

1125. ***Harmon, D. P.*** "The Public Festivals of Rome." *Aufstieg und Niedergang der roemischen Welt.* Temporini, H. and Haase, W., eds. 16, 2 (1978): 1440ff.

1126. ***Herz, P.*** "Kaiserfeste in der Prinzipatszeit." *Aufstieg und Niedergang der roemischen Welt.* Temporini, H. and Haase, W., eds. 16, 2 (1978): 1135ff.

1127. ***Juethner, J.*** "Die Augusteia in Olbasa." *WS* 24 (1902): 285-291.

1128. ***Krencker, D.*** *Das roemische Trier.* Berlin: Deutscher Kustverl., 1923.

Review: AP 1929: *Gnomon* 1929: 165-170 Dragendorff.

1129. ***Lancel, S.*** "Populus Thabarbusitanus et les Gymnasia de Quintus Flavius Lappianus." *Libyca* 6 (1958): 143-151.

1130. ***Langenfeld, H.*** "Griechische Athletinnen in der roemischen Kaiserzeit." in Renson, *The History, Evolution, and Diffusion of Sports,* pp. 116-125. See no. 137.

1131. ***Langenfeld, H.*** "Die Politik des Augustus und die griechische Agonistik." *Monumentum Chiloniense. Studien zur augusteischen Zeit. Kieler Festschrift fuer Erich Burck zum 70. Geburtstag.* Lefèvre, E., ed. Amsterdam: Hakkert, 1975: 228-259.

1131a. ***Lee, H. M.,*** "The Sport Fan and "Team" Loyalty in Ancient Rome." *Arete* 1 (1983) 139-145.

1132. ***Meusel, H.*** *Die Verwaltung und Finanzierung der oeffentlichen Baeder zur roemischen Kaiserzeit.* Diss.: University of Cologne, Cologne, 1960.

1133. ***Piernavieja, R. P.*** "Los juegos del circo en la Espana romana." *CAF* 16 (1974): 159-284.

1134. ***Regner, J.*** *"Ludi circenses." RE Suppl.* 7 (1940): coll. 1626-1664.

1135. ***Rudolph, W.*** "Der Sport in der spaetantiken Gesellschaft." *F&F* 40 (1966): 208-210.

1136. ***Ungern-Sternberg, J. von.*** "Die Einfuehrung spezieller Sitze fuer die Senatoren bei den Spielen (194 v. Chr.)." *Chiron* 5 (1975): 157ff.

1137. ***Veyne, P.*** *Le pain et le cirque. Sociologie historique d'un pluralisme politique.* Coll. l'Univers historique. Paris, Éd de Seuil, 1976.

IX

ALIEN ATTITUDES TO ATHLETICS: THE GREEKS, CHRISTIANS, AND JEWS UNDER ROME

1138. ***Arnold, I. R.*** "Agonistic Festivals in Italy and Sicily." *AJA* 64 (1960): 245-251.

1139. ***Benjamin, A. S.*** "The Altars of Hadrian in Athens and Hadrian's Panhellenic Program." *Hesperia* 32, No. 1 (1963): 57-86.

1140. ***Biers, W.*** and ***Geagen, D. J.*** "A New List of Victors in the Caesarea at Isthmia." See no. 540.

1141. ***Bishop, W. H.*** *The Role of Physical Activities in Ancient Rome.* Thesis: Univ. of Alberta, Edmonton, 1970.

1142. ***Bondolfi, A.*** "Attitudes des chrêtiens à l'égard des exercices physiques dans l'église ancienne." *Histoire de l'éducation physique et du sport.* Vol. 2, 27: 1-5. Seminar Zuerich, 1973.

1143. ***Bowersock, G. W.*** *Augustus and the Greek World.* Oxford: Clarendon Press, 1965.

Reviews: AP 1965: *REL* 43 (1965): 628-629 Richard. *LEC* 33 (1965): 464 Gilles.

1144. ***Bowersock, G. W.*** *Greek Sophists and the Roman Empire.* Oxford: Clarendon Press, 1969.

1145. ***Busch, D.*** *Er kaempfe denn recht. Sportbilder im Neuen Testament.* Zur Mitte Wuppertal Kawohl, 1972.

1146. ***Chambers, R. R.*** *Greek Athletics and the Jews, 165 B.C. -A.D. 70.* Ph. D. Diss. Miami Ohio: Miami Univ., 1980.

1147. ***Diez, E.*** "Athleten-Relief in Norikum." *Situla* 14/15 (1974): 183ff.

1148. ***Ebert, J.*** "Die lateinischen Kirchenvaeter und die antiken Wettkaempfe." *Arena (=Stadion)* 1 (1975): 185-197.

1149. ***Eisenhut, W.*** "Augustalia." *KP* 1 (1964): 740.

1150. ***Gagé, J.*** "Actiaca." *MEFR* 1936: 92-100.

1151. ***Geer, R. M.*** "The Greek Games at Naples." *TAPA* 66 (1935): 208-221.

1152. ***Gryglewicz, F.*** "Métaphores sportives chez Saint Paul." *Roczniki Teol.-Kanon* 7 (1960): 89-107.

1153. ***Harris, H. A.*** *Greek Athletics and the Jews.* Trivium Special Publ. 3. Cardiff: Univ. of Wales Pr., 1976.

Reviews: AP 1979: *CR* 29 (1979): 127-128 Rajak. AP 1977: *CW* 70 (1977): 474-475 Feldman. *G&R* 24 (1977): 96-97 Walcot. *JThS* 28 (1977): 555 Lewis. *REG* 90 (1977): 132-134 Delaygue.

1154. ***Huber, K.*** *Theorie der gymnischen Erziehung bei den Roemern.* Philosophische und paedogogische Arbeiten, V. Reihe, Heft 10 Langensalza Beyer, 1934.

Review: AP 1935: *PhW* 1935: 892-898 Schoenemann.

1155. ***Juethner, J.*** "Die Augusteia in Olbasa." See no. 1127.

1156. ***Kannengiesser, Ch.*** "Une leçon d'athlétisme. Saint Paul commenté par les Pères." *Christus* (12 rue d'Assas 75006 Paris) 85 (1975): 22-35.

1157. ***Koch, A.*** "'Leibesuebungen' im Fruehchristentum und in der beginnenden Voelkerwanderungzeit." *Geschichte der Leibesuebungen.* Ueberhorst, H., ed. vol. 2: 312-340. See no. 162.

1158. ***Koch, A.*** *Die Leibesuebungen im Urteil der antiken und fruehchristlichen Anthropologie. Ein Beitrage zur Geschichte des Sports.* Beitr. zur Lehre & Forsch. der Leibeserziehung 20. Stuttgart-Schorndorf: Hofmann, 1965.

Reviews: AP 1967: *Latomus* 26 (1967): 561 Joly. AP 1966: *Gymnasium* 73 (1966): 375-377 Mendner.

1159. ***Ladage, D.*** *"Collegia iuvenum* - Ausbildung einer municipalen Elite?" *Chiron* 9 (1979): 319-346.

1160. ***Laemmer, M.*** "Die Kaiserspiele von Caesarea im Dienste der Politik des Koenigs Herodes." *KBSW* 3. (*Jb. der Dt. Sporthochschule Koeln,* 1974). Schorndorf, 1975: 95-164.

1161. ***Langenfeld, H.*** "Griechische Athletinnen in der roemischen Kaiserzeit." in R. Renson, *History, Evolution, and Diffusion of Sports and Games in Different Cultures.*: 116-125. See no. 137.

1162. ***Meier, P. J.*** "Agon in Rom." *RE* 1 (1894): col. 866f.

1163. ***Merkelbach, R.*** "Agonistisches Epigramm aus Trajanopolis." *ZPE* 19 (1975): 301-302.

1164. ***Merkelbach, R.*** "Zu der Festordnung fuer die Sebasta in Neapel." *ZPE* 15 (1974): 192-193.

1165. ***Mohler, S. L.*** "The *iuvenes* and Roman Education." *TAPA* 68 (1937): 442-479.

1166. ***Ortega, A.*** "Metáforas del deporte griego en S. Pablo." *Helmantica* 15 (1964): 71-105.

1167. ***Petrochilos, N. K.*** *Roman Attitudes to the Greeks.* Panepist. Athenon Philos. Skhole Bibl. S. N. Saripoloy 25: Athènes, 1974.

1168. ***Pfister, G.*** *Die Erneuerung der roemischen iuventus durch Augustus.* Diss.: Regensburg, 1977.

1169. ***Pfister, G.*** "Die roemische *iuventus.*" H. Ueberhorst, ed. *Geschichte der Leibesuebungen.* vol. 2: 250-279. See no. 137.

1170. ***Pfitzner, V. C.*** "Paul and the Agon Motif. Traditional Athletic Imagery in the Pauline Literature." *NT Suppl.* 16. Leiden Brill, 1967.

1171. ***Reisch, E.*** "Aktia." *RE* 1, 1. Stuttgart, 1894: coll. 1213-1214.

1172. ***Robert, L.*** "Concours grecs en Italie. *RPh* 1930: 36-38 (=*OMS* 2: 1136-1138).

1173. ***Robert, L.*** "Deux concours grecs à Rome." *CRAI* 1 (1970): 6-27.

1174. ***Robinson, R. S.*** "Athletic Festivals in Greece and their Roman Patrons in the Second Century B.C." *Classical Studies Presented to Ben Edwin Perry by his Students and Colleagues at the University of Illinois, 1924-1960.* Illinois Stud. in Lang. & Lit. 58. Urbana: Univ. of Illinois Pr., 1969: 263-271.

1175. ***Tidman, B. M.*** "On the Foundation of the Actium Games." *CQ* 44 (1950): 123-125.

1176. ***Varjú, J.*** "A régī rómaiak nyilvános játékairól." ("Ancient Roman Public Spectacles.") *Herkules* 3 (1886): 28. sz. 8.29. sz. 5-7. 30 sz. 9-10. 31. sz. 5-6. 32. sz. 6. 34. sz. 6-7. 35. sz. 4-5. 37. sz. 5-6. 38. sz. 5-6. 41. sz. 4-5. 42. sz. 3-4.

1177. ***Varwig, R.*** "Die actischen Spiele zu Rom und Nicopolis." *Hochschulblatt fuer Leibesuebungen* 10 (1930/31): 174-178.

1178. ***Varwig, R.*** "Die Neroneen." *HfL* 10 (1930/31): 200-204.

1179. ***Varwig, R.*** "Zur Einfuehrung der griechischen Kampfspiele in Rom." *HfL* 10 (1930/31): 142-144.

1180. ***Weismann, W.*** *Kirche und Schauspiele. Die Schauspiele im Urteil der lateinischen Kirchenvaeter unter besonderer Beruecksichtigung von Augustin.* Classiciacum 27. Wuerzburg Augustinus-Verl., 1972.

Review: AP 1972: *REL* 50 (1972): 392-395 Fontaine.

1181. ***Wissowa, G.*** "Capitolia." *RE* 3 (1899): coll. 527-529.

1182. ***Zellinger, J.*** *Bad und Baeder in der altchristlichen Kirche. Eine Studie ueber Christentum und Antike.* Munich: Hueber, 1928.

Reviews: AP 1928: *HJ* 1928: 312 Weyman. *ByzZ* 1928: 196 Weyman. *RB* 1928: 383 Schmitz.

X

THE ROMAN EVENTS

A. Roman Equestrian Events

1183. ***Bianco, G.*** "Un antico cavallo di razza nella storia delle gare circensi." *RIL* 111 (1977): 313-333.
1184. ***Bronson, R. C.*** "Chariot Racing in Etruria." See no. 1083.
1185. ***Cameron, A.*** *Porphyrius the Charioteer.* Oxford: Clarendon Pr., 1973.
Reviews: AP 1973: *AC* 42 (1973): 745 Delvoye. *TLS* 72 (1973): 932.
1186. ***Floriani Squarciapino, M.*** "Circhi spettacoli circienci nelle province romane d'Africa." *RAL* 34 (1979): 275-290.
1187. ***France-Lanord, A.*** "La reconstitution du char de Vix." *CRAI* 1957: 110-113.
1188. ***Gordziejew, W.*** *Ludi scaenici et circenses.* See no. 1089.
1189. ***Lafaye, G.*** *"Equitatio."* See no. 901.
1190. ***Martin, A.*** *"Equites."* See no. 904.
1191. ***Matz, D.*** "Charioteers and Gladiators. Some Comparisons Based on the Epigraphical Evidence." See no. 1211.
1192. ***Nachod, H.*** *Der Rennwagen bei den Italikern und ihren Nachbarn.* Diss.: Leipzig: Radelli & Hille, 1909.
1193. ***Nuoffer, O.*** *Der Rennwagon im Altertum.* See no. 908.
1194. ***Palmieri, R.*** "Ricordi di ludi circienses a Teanum Sidicinum." *RAAN* 53 (1978): 57-65.
1195. ***Saglio, E.*** "Desultor." *D.-S.* 2, 1. Paris, 1892: 111-113.
1196. ***Schneider, K.*** "Quadriga." See no. 925.
1197. ***Syme, R.*** "Scorpus the charioteer." *AJAH* 2(1977): 86-94.
1198. ***Thomas, M.*** "Ovid at the Races." See no. 1578.
1199. ***Turner, E. G.*** "The Charioteers from Antinoe." *JHS* 93 (1973): 192-195. 5th-6th c. A.D. papyrus fragment.

B. Gladiators and *Venationes*

1200. ***Amelotti, M.*** "La posizione degli atleti di fronte al diritto romano." *SDHI* 21 (1955): 123ff.
1201. ***Blázquez, J. M.*** "Venationes y juegos de toros en la antiguedad." *Zephyrus* 13 (1962): 47-65.

1202. ***Blázquez-Martínez, J. M.*** "Representaticiònes de gladiadores en el Museo Arqueológico Nacional." *Zephyrus* 9 (1958): 79-94.

1203. ***Faccenna, D.*** "Relievi gladiatorii." *BMCR* 19 (1956-1958): 37-75.

1204. ***Frisch, P.*** "Inschrift fuer einen Gladiator aus Alexandria Troas." *ZPE* 13 (1974): 111.

1205. ***Gabelmann, H.*** "Circusspiele in der spaetantiken Repraesentationskunst." *AW* 10, 4 (1980): 25-38.

1206. ***Gansiniec, Z.*** "Les gladiateurs." (in Polish) *Filomata* 153 (1961): 227-236.

1207. ***Grant, M.*** *Gladiators.* London: Weidenfeld and Nicholson; Penguin, 1967.

Reviews: *AP* 1972: *Akroterion* 17, 2-3 (1972): 30-31 Marity. *AP* 1969: *Phoenix* 23 (1969): 233-24 Baldwin. *AP* 1968: *G&R* 15 (1968): 204 Sewter. German translation, *Die Gladiatoren,* von Mannsperger, B. and Schmalzriedt, E., transs. Stuttgart: Klett, 1970. Reviews: *AP* 1971: *AKG* 53 (1971): 171-172 Meyer. *AP* 1970: *BO* 27 (1970): 416.

1208. ***Grant, M.*** "The Gladiators." *HT* 17 (1967): 610-617.

1209. ***Kokolakis, M.*** "Gladiatorial games and animal-baiting in Lucian." *Platon* 10 (1958): 328-351.

1210. ***Lafaye, G.*** "Venatio.' *D.-S.* 5. Paris, 1914: 680-711.

1211. ***Matz, D.*** "Charioteers and Gladiators. Some Comparisons Based on the Epigraphical Evidence." *CB* 56 (1980): 37-39.

1212. ***Neppi-Modona, A.*** "Frustula gladiatoria." *Hommages à A. Grenier.* Renard, M., ed. Coll. Latomus 58. Berchen-Bruxelles 61 Av. Laure, 1962: 1185-1187.

1213. ***Neppi-Modona, A.*** *Gli edifici teatrali greci e romani. Teatri, odei, anfiteatri, circhi.* Florence: Olschki, 1961.

Reviews: AP 1961: *Athenaeum* 39 (1961): 379-380 Polacco. *Dioniso* 35, 2 (1961): 101-102 Caputo.

1214. ***Pearson, J.*** *Arena. The Story of the Colosseum.* New York: McGraw Hill, 1973.

1215. ***Robert, L.*** *Les gladiateurs dans l'Orient grec.* Amsterdam: Hakkert, 1971. Photographic reprint of 1940 edition.

Reviews: *StudClas* 14 (1972): 339-340 Pippidi. AP 1971: *CRAI* 1971: 500 Robert.

1216. ***Sabbatini, Tumolesi Longo P.*** "Doccumenti gladiatori dell'Occidente romano, I: Iscrizioni dell'età repubblicana." *RAL* 29 (1974): 283-292.

1217. ***Sabbatini, Tumulosi Longo P.*** "Gladiatoria, I." *RAL* 26 (1971): 735-749.

1218. ***Sabbatini, Tumulosi Longo P.*** "Gladiatoria, IV." *RAL* 27 (1972): 485-495.

1219. ***Sabbatini, Tumolesi Longo P.*** *Gladiatorum paria. Annunci di spettacoli gladiatoria Pompeii.* Tituli I. Rome: Ed. di Storia e Lett., 1980.

1220. ***Sceglov, A. N.*** "Sur la question des combats de gladiateurs à Chersonèse de Tauride." (in Russian) *Eirene* 5 (1966): 99-105.

1221. ***Schneider, K.*** *"Gladiatores." RE Suppl.* 3 (1918): 760-784.

1222. ***Stekelendurg, A. V. van.*** "Die romeinse gladiatore." *Akroterion* 19, 4 (1974): 14-23.

1223. ***Stekelenburg, A. V. van.*** "Die romeinse gladiatore." *Akroterion* 20, 2-3 (1975): 28-37.

1224. ***Toynbee, J. M. C.*** *Death and Burial in the Roman World.* Aspects of Greek & Roman Life. Ithaca: Cornell Univ. Pr., 1971.

Reviews: AP 1971: *G&R* 18 (1971): 234 Sewter. *JRS* 61 (1971): 283-284 Green. *Mod. Lang. Journ.* 55 (Nat. Fed. of Mod. Lang. Teachers, Boulder, Colo.) (1971): 483-484 Thurman.

1225. ***Venedkov, I.*** 'Le mors thrace." (in Bulgarian with French summary) *BIAB* 21 (1957): 153-201.

1226. ***Ville, G.*** "Les jeux de gladiateurs dans l'empire chrétien." *MEFR* 72 (1960): 273-335.

1227. ***Wahl, J.*** "Gladiatorenhelm-Beschlaege vom Limes." *Germania* 55 (1977): 108-132.

1228. ***Weismann, W.*** "Gladiator." *RLAC* 11 (1979) Lief. 81: 23-45.

C. Miscellaneous Roman Sports and Games

1229. ***Aymard, J.*** "Quelques remarques sur les jeux avec le taureau à l'époque romaine." *LEC* 23 (1955): 259-266.

1230. ***Bendala, Galán, M.*** "Tablas de Juego en Itálica." *Habis* 4 (1973): 263-272.

1231. ***Butler, A. J.*** *Sport in Classic Times.* See no. 997.

1232. ***Cameron, A.*** "Sex in the Swimming Pool." *BICS* 20 (1973): 149-150.

1233. ***Feriz, H.*** "Nogmaals de Geknevelde Stier." *Hermeneus* 36 (1964): 11.

1234. ***Foucher, L.*** "Nemesis, le griffon et les jeux d'amphithéâtre." *Mélanges d'histoire ancienne offerts à William Seston.* Publ. de la Sorbonne Sér. Études 9. Paris: de Boccard, 1974: 187-195.

1235. ***Lafaye, G.*** *"Pila."* See no. 967.

1236. ***Mau.*** "Ballspiel." See no. 968.

1237. ***Mau.*** *"Expulsim."* See no. 970.

1238. ***Mau.*** *"Follis."* See no. 971.

1239. ***Mehl, E.*** "Turnkunst." See no. 1015.

1240. ***Mendner, S.*** *Das Ballspiel im Leben der Voelker.* See no. 972.
1241. ***Mendner, S.*** "Gesellschaftspiele." See no. 973.
1242. ***Mendner, S.*** "Das Spiel Phaininda-Harpastum." See no. 974.
1243. ***Mitchell, L. B.*** "Ancient Ball Games." See no. 976.
1244. ***Mohler, S. L.*** *The Cestus.* See no. 853.
1245. ***Orth, E.*** "Jagd." See no. 1020.
1246. ***Picard, G. Ch.*** "A propos de la mosaïque des taureaux découverte à El-Diem." *BCTH* 1957 (1959): 106-113.
1247. ***Radke, G.*** "*Trigon.*" *RE* 7 A, 1. Stuttgart, 1939: col. 139.
1248. ***Rattenbury, R. M.*** "How to Toss a Bull." *PCPhS* 178 (1941-1945): 14.
1249. ***Tilander, G.*** *Cynegtica.* See no. 1031.
1250. ***Traversari, G.*** *Gli spettacoli in acqua nel teatro tardoantico.* Rome: L'Erma, 1960.
Reviews: AP 1960: *Athenaeum* 38 (1960): 359-361 Frova. *REL* 38 (1960): 485-486 Lantier.
1251. ***Turner, R. C.*** "A Roman Gaming Board from near Bownesson-Solway." *TCWA* 80 (1980): 159.
1252. ***Wegner, E.*** *Das Ballspiel der Roemer.* Diss.: Rostock, 1938.
1253. ***Weyens, P.*** "Het Ballspiel in de klassieke oudheid." See no. 990.
1254. ***Wilhelm, H. E.*** "Faustball bei den Roemern?" *LKE* 53 (1934): 369-370.
1255. ***Young, N.*** "Did the Greeks and Romans Play Football?" See no. 992.

D. Roman Aquatic Sports

1256. ***Mehl, E.*** *Antike Schwimmkunst.* See no. 942.
1257. ***Mehl, E.*** "Schwimmen." See no. 945.
1258. ***Mehl, E.*** "Warum bevorzugen die antiken Kulturvoelker das Schlagschwimen...?" See no. 947.
1259. ***Sanders, H. A.*** "Swimming among the Greeks and Romans." See no. 952.
1260. ***Strempel, R.*** "Schwimmen und Voltigieren im alten Rom. Uebersetzung und Betrachtung nach der *epitoma rei militaris* des Flavius Vegetius Renatus." *HfL* 10 (1930): 30-33.
1261. ***Tilley, A. F.*** "An Experiment under Oars." See no. 956.
1262. ***Tilley, A. F.*** and ***Fenwick, V. H.*** "Rowing in the Mediterranean." See no. 957.
1263. ***Traversari, G.*** *Gli spettacoli in acqua nel teatro tardoantico.* See no. 1250.

XI

ROMAN BATHS

1264. ***Cunliffe, B.*** *Roman Bath discovered.* London: Routledge & Kegan Paul, 1971.

Review: AP 1971: *G&R* 18 (1971): 232 Sewter.

1265. ***Fine-Licht, K. de.*** *Untersuchungen an den Traiansthermen zu Rom. ARID* 7 Suppl. Copenhagen: Munksgaard, 1974.

1266. ***Grunauer, S.*** "Thermen und oeffentlicher Badebetrieb." *Altsprachlicher Unterricht* 20, 3 (1977): 49ff.

1267. ***Krencker, D.*** "Die Kaiserthermen in Trier und roemische Thermen im allgemeinen." *WB* 1929: 19-20. Cf. *F&F* 4 (1928): 93.

1268. ***Krencker, D.; Krueger, H.; Lehmann, H.*** **and** ***Wachtler, H.*** *Die Trierer Kaiserthermen, Abt I: Ausgrabungsber. und grundsaetzliche Untersuchungen roemischer Thermen.* Augsburg: Filser, 1929.

Reviews: AP 1929: *JRS* 1929: 103-104. *LZB* 1929: 1193.

1269. ***Mau.*** "Baeder." *RE* 2, 2. Stuttgart, 1896: coll. 2743-2758.

1270. ***Muesel, H.*** *Die Verwaltung und Finanzierung der oeffentlichen Baeder zur roemischen Kaiserzeit.* See no. 1132.

1271. ***Micca, B. A.*** "Il bagno presso i Romani." *Minerva medica* 29, 1 No. 6 (1938): 1-8.

1272. ***Neppi-Modona, A.*** "Ricerche su alcuni termini relativi ai ludi circensi." *Hommages à L. Herrmann:* Coll. Latomus. Berchem-Bruxelles, 61 Av. Laure, 1960: 562-570.

XII

ATHLETICS IN ART AND ARCHAEOLOGY

A. General

1273. ***Amandry, P.*** "A propos de Polyclète: Statues d'Olympioniques et carrière de sculpteurs." *Charites. Studien zur Altertumswissenschaft.* Dedicated to E. Langlotz; ed by K. von Schauenberg. Bonn, 1957: 63-87.

1274. ***Bargellini, P.*** Die Kunst der Etrusker. See no. 1079.

1275. ***Bartoccini, R., Lerici, C. M.*** and ***Moretti, M.*** *Tarquinia. La tomba delle olimpiadi.* See no. 1080.

1276. ***Beazley, J. D.*** *Attic Black-figure Vase-painters.* Oxford, 1956. Pages 403-417 on Panathenaic amphorae.

1277. ***Beazley, J. D.*** *The Development of Attic Black-figure.* Berkeley and L.A.: U. Cal. Press, 1964. Pages 88-100 on Panathenaic amphorae.

1278. ***Beazley, J. D.*** "A Hoplitodromos Cup." See no. 636.

1279. ***Beazley, J. D.*** "Panathenaica." *AJA* 47, No. 4 (1943): 441-465.

1280. ***Beazley, J. D.*** *Paralipomena.* (supplements *Attic Black-figure Vase-painters.)* Oxford, 1971. Page 175 on Panathenaic amphorae.

1281. ***Becatti, G.*** "Un grupo ostiense di lottatori." See no. 812.

1282. ***Benedum, J.*** "Ohrverletzungen an Athleten auf Darstellung des Altertums und ihre Beziehung zur medizinischen Literatur der Zeit." *Gesnerus* 25 (1968): 11-28.

1283. ***Bernardini, M.*** "Vasi a sogetto sportivo nel Museo di Lecce." *StudSal* 9-10 (1960): 5-22.

1284. ***Bernhard, O.*** "Leibesuebungen und Koerperflege im Gymnasion auf Muenzen." *Koepererziehung* 9 (1933): 110-115.

1285. ***Bieber, M.*** *The History of the Greek and Roman Theater.* Princeton: Princeton U. Press and London: Oxford, Press, 1961. Includes discussion of amphitheater.

1286. ***Bloch, R.*** *Die Kunst der Etrusker.* See no. 1082.

1287. ***Bluemel, C.*** *Sport der Hellenen.* See no. 12.

1288. ***Bluemel, C.*** *Sport und Spiel bei Griechen und Roemern. Bildwerke aus den Staatlichen Museen zu Berlin.* Berlin: Verl. fuer Kunstwissenschaft, 1934.

1289. ***Boardman, J.*** *Athenian Black Figure Vases.* Oxford, 1974. Page 211 on Athletic vases.

1290. ***Boardman, J.*** *Athenian Red Figure Vases: The Archaic Period.* Oxford, 1974. Page 220 on athletic vases.

1291. ***Boethius, A.*** and ***Ward-Perkins, J. B.*** *Etruscan and Roman Architecture.* N. Y.: Pelican Books, 1973.[3] Includes amphitheaters and baths.

1292. ***Borthwick, E. K.*** "The Gymnasium of Bromius - a Note on Dionysus Chaleus, fr. 3." *JHS* 84 (1964): 320-330.

1293. ***Brauchitsch, G. v.*** *Die panathenaische Preisamphoren.* Leipzig, 1910.

1294. ***Broneer, O.*** "An Archaeological Enigma." *Archaeology* 9 (1956): 134-137.

1295. ***Broneer, O.*** "The Enigma Explained." *Archaeology* 9 (1956): 268-272.

1296. ***Broneer, O.*** "Starting Devices in Greek Stadia." See no. 640.

1297. ***Bruchner, A.*** *Palaestradarstellungen auf fruehrotfigurigen attischen Vasen.* Diss.: Basel (Hannover), 1954.

1298. ***Burkhardt, H. W.*** *Reitertypen auf griechishen Vasen.* Diss.: Munich,1906.

1299. ***Buschor, E.*** "Sport und Kunst der Griechen." *LKE* 55 (1936): 353-358 + Abb. 2-17. S. I-IV.

1300. ***Caskey, L. D.*** "Brygos as a Painter of Athletic Scenes." *AJA* 19 (1915): 129-136.

1301. ***Casson, S.*** "The New Athenian Statue Bases." *JHS* 45 (1925): 164-179.

1302. ***Colagrossi, P.*** *L'anfiteatro flavio.* Florence: Libreria Editrice, 1913.

1303. ***Della, Seta, A.*** "Base di statua con relievi arcaici scoperta in Atene." *Dedalo* 3 (1922): 207-226.

1304. ***Della, Seta, A.*** "Un'altra base ateniese con rilievi arcaici." *Dedalo* 3 (1922): 409-423.

1305. ***Delorme, J.*** *Gymnasion. Étude sur les monuments consacrés à l'éducation en Grèce (des origines à l'empire romain.)* Paris, 1960.

1306. **Diez, E.** "Ein roemerzeitliches Athletenbild in der Steiermark." *Festschrift des Instituts fuer Leibeserziehung der Univ. Graz.*, 1973. vol. 2: 15ff.

1307. ***Dihl, M.*** "Zum Diskobol des Myron." See no. 733.

1308. ***Dorigny, S.*** "Stadium." *D.-S.* 4, 2. Paris, s. a.: 1449-1456.

1309. ***Dow, S.*** "Panathenaic Amphorae from the Hellenistic Period." *Hesperia* 5, No. 1 (1936): 50-58. On Panathenaic amphorae and Hellenistic prizes.

1310. ***Drees, L.*** *Olympia: Gods, Artists, and Athletes.* See no. 332.

1311. ***Durm, J.*** *Handbuch der Architektur.* Volume II, *Die Baukunst der Roemer.* Stuttgart: Kroener, 1905.

1312. ***Edwards, G. R.*** "Panathenaics of Hellenistic and Roman Times." *Hesperia* 26, No. 3 (1957): 320-349.

1313. ***Fiechter, E.*** "Stadion (der Bau)." *RE* 3 A, 2. Stuttgart, 1929: coll. 1967-1973.

1314. ***Fougères, G.*** "Gymnasium." *D.-S.* 2, 2. Paris, 1896: 1689-1698.

1315. ***Frel, Jiri.*** *Panathenaic Prize Amphoras.* Kerameikos Book no. 2. Athens, 1973.

1316. ***Gabelmann, H.*** "Circusspiele in der spaetantiken Repraesentationskunst." See no. 1205.

1317. ***Gardner, P.*** "The Apoxyomenos of Lysippus." *JHS* 25 (1905): 234-259.

1318. ***Gardner, P.*** "A Stele Commemorating a Victory in a Boat Race." See no. 937.

1319. ***Gardiner, E. N.*** "Athletics and Art." *Athletics of the Ancient World.* pp. 53-71. See no. 40.

1320. ***Gardiner, E. N.*** "Panathenaic Amphorae.' See no. 565.

1321. ***Gentili, G. V.*** "Studi e ricerche sull'anfiteatro di Siracusa." See no. 1121.

1322. ***Gerhard, E.; Klugemann, A.*** and ***Koerte, G.*** *Etruskische Spiegel.* See no. 1087.

1323. ***Glass, S. L.*** *Palaistra and Gymnasium in Greek Architecture.* Diss.: Univ. of Pennsylvania, 1967.
Summary: AP 1968: *DA* 29 (1968): 204A.

1324. ***Greco, F.*** *L'educazione fisica nella poesia, nella letterature e nell'arte greca.* Bologna: Casa ed. Ponte Nuovo, 1962.
Review: AP 1964: *RBPh* 42 (1964): 1474 Lesuisse.

1325. ***Gross, W. H.*** "Siegerstatuen." *KP* 5 (1975): 178-179.

1326. ***Gross, W. H.*** "Quos iconicas vocant." See no. 346.

1327. ***Gruendel, L.*** *Die Darstellung des Laufens in der griechischen Kunst.* See no. 648.

1328. ***Harris, H. A.*** "Athletics in Greek Art." Summary of paper in *PCA* 53 (1966): 25-26.

1329. ***Harris, H. A.*** "Stadia and Starting-grooves." *G&R* 7 (1960): 25-35.

1330. ***Harris, H. A.*** "The Starting Gate for Chariots at Olympia." See no. 894.

1331. ***Harris, H. A.*** "The Starting Gate...A Postscript." See no. 893.

1332. ***Hekler, A.*** "Marmortorso einer Athletenstatue in Budapest." *JDAI* 31 (1916): 95-104.

1333. ***Henze, A.*** "Die antike Architektur vollendete sich im roemischen Sportbau." *AW* 1 (1970, 2): 30-35. Includes sports architecture.

1334. ***Hook, L. van.*** "An Athlete Relief from the Themistoclean Wall, Athens." *AJA* 30 (1926): 283-287.

1335. ***Humphreys, S. C.*** "Artists' mistakes." *IJNA* 7 (1978): 78-79.

1336. ***Hyde, W. W.*** *De olympionicarum statuis a Pausanii commemoratis.* See no. 359.

1337. ***Hyde, W. W.*** *Olympic Victor Monuments and Greek Athletic Art.* See no. 484.

1338. ***Hyde, W. W.*** "The Oldest Dated Victor Statue." *AJA* 18, No. 2 (1914): 156-164.

1339. ***Hyde, W. W.*** "The Positions of Victor Statues at Olympia." *AJA* 16, No. 2 (1912): 203-229.

1340. ***Hyde, W. W.*** "Were Olympic Victor Statues Exclusively of Bronze?" *AJA* 19, No. 1 (1915): 57-62.

1341. ***Jerace, M.*** *La Ginnastica nei suoi rapporti con l'arte greca.* Florence/Turin/Rome, 1899.

1342. ***Juethner, J.*** "Verzeichnete Athletendarstellungen auf Vasen." *Oesterr. Jahresh.* 31 (1938): 1-18.

1343. ***Kalkmann, A.*** "Die Statue von Subiaco." *JDAI* 10 (1895): 46ff.

1344. ***Kietz, G.*** *Agonistische Studien. 1. Der Diskuswerf bei den Griechen und seine kuenstlerischen Motive.* See no. 743.

1345. ***Korti-Konti, S.*** "Onlookers in the Representations of Deeds and Games in Ancient Greek Art." *EEThess* 18 (1979): 167-205.

1346. ***Lamb, W.*** "Seven Vases from the Hope Collection." *JHS* 38 (1918): 27-36.

1347. ***Lange, K.*** "Sportdarstellungen auf griechischen Muenzen." *Olympische Rundschau* H. 14 (1951): 1-5 + Tab. 1-3. Abbild. nr. 1-15.

1348. ***Legakis, B.*** *Athletic Contests in Archaic Greek Art.* Diss. U. Chicago, 1977.

1349. ***Legakis, B.*** "Nicosthenic Athletics," in *Ancient Ceramics in the J. Paul Getty Museum.* Malibu, 1973. Primarily on boxing.

1350. ***Lisicar, P.*** "Les strigiles des collections yougoslaves." (in Croatian with French summary) *ZAnt* 8 (1958): 323-331.

1351. ***McDaniel, W. B.*** "The So-Called Athlete's Ring." *AJA* 22, No. 3 (1918): 295-303. (speculates on its use for olive pressing.)

1352. ***McDaniel, W. B.*** "The So-Called Bow Puller of Antiquity." *AJA* 22, No. 1 (1918): 25-43. (part of headset for horses.)

1353. ***Miliadhis, Y.*** "The Charioteer of Delphi." *Greek Heritage* 1, No. 2 (1964): 12-14.

1354. ***Moestue, W.*** "Die griechische Ablaufbezirke." See no. 670.

1355. ***Moestue, W.*** "Griechische Ablaufstellungen und Ablaufvorgaenge." See no. 671.

1356. ***Moestue, W.*** "Die griechische Laufbahnen." See no. 672.

1357. ***Moestue, W.*** "Die Sportflaeche im griechischen Stadion." *Die Leibesuebungen 9 (1933): 103-107.*

1358. ***Moestue, W.*** "Mallinien, Wendeschranken und Zielbezirke im griechischen Stadion." See no. 673.

1359. ***Moretti, L.*** "Lo scultore Akestor." *ArchClass* 7 (1955): 187-189.

1360. ***Moretti, M.*** and ***Matt, L. von.*** *Etruskische Malerei in Tarquinia.* See no. 1099.

1361. ***Mylonas, G. E.*** "The Bronze Statue from Artemision." *AJA* 48 (1944): 143-160. Discussion of "Zeus Artemision" statue as not being that of a javelin thrower.

1362. ***Napoli, M.*** "Le Pitture greche della tomba del Tuffatore." *Le Scienze* aprile 1969: 9-19.

1363. ***Neppi-Modona, A.*** *Gli edifici teatrali Greci e Romani.* Florence: Olschki, 1951.

1364. ***Neutsch, B.*** *Der Sport im Bilde griechischer Kunst.* Willsbach-Heidelberg: Scherer Verl., 1949.

1365. ***Paolo, A. di; Vighi, R.; Passamonti, R.; Spaini, A.; Volpicelli, L.*** and ***Jannatori, L.*** *Le livre des Jours italiens.* (On sport in ancient art.) Rome: E.N.L.T., 1960. Review: AP 1960: *REL* 38 (1960): 483 Chevallier.

1366. ***Patrucco, R.*** *Lo stadio di Epidauro.* Rome.

1367. ***Petersen, Ch.*** *Das gymnasium der Griechen.* See no. 120.

1368. ***Philadelpheus, A.*** "Bases Archaïques Trouvées dans le mur de Thémistocle à Athènes." *BCH* 46 (1922): 1-35.

1369. ***Philadelpheus, A.*** "Báseis met' anaglýphon artíos aneuretheĩsai en Athénais." *Arkh. Deltion* 6 (1920-1921): 1-20.

1370. ***Philadelpheus, A.*** "Reliefs von attischen Statuebasen." *AA* 1922: coll. 56-59.

1371. ***Philadelpheus, A.*** "Three Statue-Bases Recently Discovered at Athens." *JHS* 42 (1922): 104-106.

1372. ***Polacco, L.*** *L'atleta Cirene-Perinto.* Rome, 1955.

1373. ***Potter, J.*** *Archaeologica Graeca or the Antiquities of Greece I.* Edinburgh, 1827.

1374. ***Preedy, J. B. K.*** "The Chariot Group of the Maussoleum." *JHS* 30, Part 1 (1910): 133-162.

1375. ***Putnam, B. J.*** *Concepts of Sport in Minoan Art.* Diss.: Univ. of Southern California, 1967.
Summary: AP 1968: *DA* 28 (1968): 4975A.

1376. ***Quennell, Peter.*** *The Colosseum.* N. Y.: Newsweek Publications, 1971.

1377. ***Robert, L.*** "Monuments des gladiateurs dans l'orient grec." *Hellenica* 3 (1946): 112-150; 5 (1948): 77-99; 7 (1949): 126-151; 8 (1950): 39-72.

1378. ***Robert, L.*** "Un athlète Milésien." See no. 626.

1379. ***Robertson, M.*** "A Fragment by the Nikoxenos Painter." *AJA* 66 (1962): 311-312.

1380. ***Rocchetti, L.*** "Il mosaico con scene d'arena al Museo Borghese." *RIA* 10 (1961): 79-115.

1380a. ***Romano, D. G.***, *The Stadia of the Peloponnesos.* Diss.: U. Pa., 1981.

1380b. ***Romano, D. G.***, "The Ancient Stadium: Athletes and Arete," *AncW* 7 (1983) 9-16.

1381. ***Rudolph, W.*** "Bemerkungen zu Sportdarstellungen auf Vasenbildern." *WZ* Rostock 16 (1967): 507-510.

1382. ***Scherer, Ch.*** *De Olympionicarum statuis.* See no. 427.

1383. ***Schneider, K.*** *Die griechischen Gymnasien und Palaistren nach ihrer geschichtlichen Entwicklung.* 1908.

1384. ***Schroeder, B.*** "Der antike Sport in der bildenden Kunst." Vort. geh. in der Versamml. der Freunde des hym. Gymn. in Oldenburg: *HG* 1932: 157 Gabler.

1385. ***Schroeder, B.*** *Zum Diskobol des Myron.* See no. 750.

1386. ***Schweitzer, B.*** "Der Diskoswerfer der Glyptothek in Muenchen." *Die Antike* 15 (1939): 271-274.

1387. ***Sieveking, J.*** "Zum Myronischen Diskobol." See no. 754.

1388. ***Strohmeyer, H.*** "Die Leibesuebungen in der Situlenkunst." See no. 1106.

1389. ***Suemeghy, V.*** "Das Problem des Myronischen Diskobol." See no. 756.

1390. ***Thouvenot, R.*** "Sur deux statuettes de gladiateurs du Maroc romain." *Hommages à L. Herrmann.* Coll. Latomus 44. Burchem-Bruxelles, 61 Av. Laure, 1960: 715-721.

1391. ***Thurneyessen, J.*** "Artists' Mistakes. A Reply." *IJNA* 8 (1979): 254.

1392. ***Turner, E. G.*** "The Charioteers from Antinoe." *JHS* 93 (1973): 192-195. A 5th-6th c. A. D. papyrus fragment.

1393. ***Uhlig, M.*** "Zum Diskuswerfer des Myron." See no. 758.

1394. ***Van Mercklin, E.*** "Chariots on Geometric Vases." See no. 928.

1395. ***Vighi, R.*** *Sporte et Arte. Trecentocinquanta opera dalla mostra dello Sport nella Storia e nell'arte.* Rome, 1960.

1396. ***Vighi, R.*** *Lo sport nella storia e nell'arte. Mostra retrospettiva di documentazioni sportive in Italia dall'antichità al sec. 19.* Rome: Tipogr. artist., 1960.
Review: AP 1961: *Latomus* 20 (1961): 440.

1397. ***Wace, A. J. B.*** "Recent Excavations in Asia Minor." *JHS* 23 (1903): 335-355.

1398. ***Waldstein, C.*** "Pythagoras of Rhegion and the Early Athlete Statues I." *JHS* 1 (1880): 168-201.

1399. ***Waldstein, C.*** "Pythagoras of Rhegion and the Early Athlete Statues II." *JHS* 2 (1881): 332-351.

1400. ***Washburn, O. M.*** "The Charioteer of Amphion at Delphi." *AJA* 12, No. 2 (1908): 198-208.

1401. ***Washburn, O. M.*** "The Charioteer of Delphi." *AJA* 10, No. 2 (1908): 151-153.

1402. ***Young, C. H.*** "A Bronze Statuette in the Metropolitan Museum of Art." *AJA* 30 (1926): 427-431.

1403. ***Young, R. S.*** "Late Geometric Graves and a Seventh Century Wall in the Agora." *Hesperia* Suppl. 2 (1939): 1-235.

1404. ***Zschietzschmann, W.*** "Gymnasion." *KP* 1 (1967): 887.

1405. ***Zschietschmann, W.*** *Wettkampf- und Uebungsstaetten in Griechenland. Stadion, Palaestra, Gymnasion. Eine Uebersicht, 2: Palaestra, Gymnasion.* Beitraege zur Lehre u. Forschung der Leibeserziehung 8. Schorndorf bei Stuttgart, 1961.

B. Inscriptions

1406. ***Aupert, P.*** "*Athletica I:* Épigraphie archaïque et morphologie des stade anciens." *BCH* 104 (1980): 309-315.

1407. ***Bizard, L.*** "Fouilles de Ptoion (1903) - II. Inscriptions." *BCH* 44 (1920): 227-262.

1407a. ***Clay, D.***, "A Gymnasium Inventory from the Athenian Agora," *Hesperia* 46 (1977): 259-269.

1408. ***Daux, G.*** "Décret d'Ephèse pour un vanquer aux Isthme et aux Nemea." See no. 538.

1409. ***Daux, G.*** "Sur quelques inscriptions (anthroponymes, concours à Pergame, serment éphébique)." See no. 584.

1410. ***Dittenberger, W.*** and ***Purgold, K.*** *Die Inschriften von Olympia.* See no. 472.

1411. ***Dow, S.*** and ***Oliver, J. H.*** "Greek Inscriptions." *Hesperia* 4, No. 1 (1935): 1-107.

1412. ***Dunst, G.*** "Die Inschrift des Periodoniken Leon." See no. 815.

1413. ***Ebert, J.*** "Epigraphische Miszellen." *WZ Halle* 16 (1967): 411-417.

1414. ***Ebert, J.*** "Das Epigramm fuer Hagesistratos von Rhodes." See no. 840.

1415. ***Ebert, J.*** *Griech. Epigramme auf Seiger an Gymnischen und hippischen Agonen.* Abh. der Saechs. Akad. der Wiss. philol.-hist. Kl. 63, 2. Berlin: Akad.-Verl., 1972.

1416. ***Ebert, J.*** "Zu griechischen agonistischen Epigrammen." *WZ Halle* 14 (1965): 95-100.

1417. ***Ebert, J.*** "Zu griechischen agonistischen Inschriften." *WZ Halle* 15 (1966): 375-387.

1418. ***Ebert, J.*** "Zu griechischen Siegerepigrammen." *WZ Halle* 15 (1966): 389-400.

1419. ***Ebert, J.*** "Zu vier agonistischen Epigrammen." *APF* 19 (1969): 140-146.

1420. ***Frisch, P.*** "Inschrift fuer einen Gladiator aus Alexandria Troas." *ZPE* 13 (1974): 111.

1421. ***Guarducci, M.*** "Tre iscrizioni archaice di Corintho. 3. L'altere dell'Istmo." See no. 700.

1422. ***Harris, H. A.*** "Notes on Three Athletic Inscriptions." *JHS* 82 (1962): 19-24.

1423. ***Harris, H. A.*** "An Olympic Epigram." See no. 481.

1424. ***Iacopi, G.*** "Iscrizione Greca." *NSA* 1952: 167-176.

1424a. ***Jordan, D. R.*** and ***Spawforth, J. S.,*** "A New Document from the Isthmian Games." See no. 539a.

1424b. ***Kent, J. H.,*** *Corinth.* See no. 539b.

1425. ***Klee, Th.*** *Zur Geschichte der gymnischen Agone an griechischen Festen.* See no. 75.

1426. ***Laemmer, M.*** *Die Bedeutung epigraphischer Zeugnisse fuer die Geschichte der griechischen Gymnastik und Agonistik.* Koeln Hist. Semin. der Dt. Sporthochschule, 1968: 21-58.

1427. ***Masow, H. von.*** "Die stele des Ainetos in Amyklai." See no. 604.

1427a. ***Meritt, B. D.,*** *Corinth.* See no. 540a.

1428. ***Meritt, B. D.*** "Greek Inscriptions." See no. 570.

1429. ***Meritt, B. D.*** "Greek Inscriptions." See no. 571.

1430. ***Meritt, B. D.*** "Greek Inscriptions." *Hesperia* 29, No. 1 (1960): 1-86. Concerning a paidotribe.

1431. ***Merkelbach, R.*** "Ueber ephesisches Dekret fuer einen Athletentitel *Paradoxos.*" See no. 605.

1432. ***Merkelbach, R.*** "Agonistisches Epigramm aus Trajanopolis." See no. 1163.

1433. ***Merkelbach, R.*** "Nachmals zur Dekret fuer den Pankratisten Kallikrates." See no. 877.

1434. ***Mie, F.*** "Ueber *dià pânton und ho epiníkios* in agonistischen Inschriften." *MDAI(A)* 34 (1909): 1-22.

1435. ***Mitsos, M.*** "Eine agonistische Inschrift aus Argos." See no. 606.

1436. ***Moestue, W.*** "Die Frage der griechischen Ablauf-Sperrschranken. Eine kritische Studie." *HfL* 11 (1932): 375-377.

1437. ***Moretti, L.*** *Iscrizioni Agonistiche Greche.* Rome, 1953.

1438. ***Moretti, L.*** *Olympionikai,* and "Supplemento degli Olympionikai." See nos. 402 and 403.

1439. ***Morissey, E. J.*** "Victors in the Prytaneion Decree." See no. 907.

1440. ***Peek, W.*** "Vier Grabgedichte auf einem Paidotriben aus Hermupolis Magna." *WZ Halle* 11 (1962): 993-1013.

1441. ***Piernavieja, Rozitis P.*** "Lápidas deportivas inéditas." *AEA* 44 (1971): 160-164.

1442. ***Pugliese, Carratelli G.*** "Supplemento epigrafico rodio." *ASAA* 30-32 (1952-1954): 247-316.

1443. ***Reinmuth, O. W. R.*** *The Ephebic Inscriptions of the Fourth Century B. C.* See no. 308.

1444. ***Reinmuth, O. W. R.*** "Ephebic Texts from Athens." *Hesperia* 30, No. 1 (1961): 8-22. (paidotribes, gymnasium, and gymnastic training.)

1445. ***Reinmuth, O. W. R.*** "The Ephebic Inscription, Athenian agora I 285." *Hesperia* 24, No. 3 (1955): 220-239.

1446. ***Reynolds, J.*** and ***Mason, O.*** "Une inscription éphébique de Ptolemais (Cyrenaique)." See no. 310.

1447. ***Richter, G. M.*** "Another Archaic Greek Mirror." *AJA* 46, No. 3 (1942): 319-324. Possible Spartan female athlete.

1448. ***Richter, G. M.*** "An Archaic Greek Mirror." *AJA* 42, No. 3 (1938): 337-344. Also in *BMM* 1942: 150-152. Possible Spartan female athlete.

1449. ***Riele, G. J. M. J. te.*** "Inscriptions conservées au Musée d'Olympie." *BCH* 88 (1964): 169-195.

1450. ***Ringwood, Irene C.*** *Agonistic Features of Local Greek Festivals Chiefly from Inscriptional Evidence.* See no. 612.

1451. ***Robert, L.*** "Base d'une statue d'athlète." *BCH* 49 (1925): 232-233 (=*OMS* 1: 26-27.)

1452. ***Robert, L.*** "Deux inscriptions agonistiques de Rhodes." See no. 619.

1453. ***Robert, L.*** "Epigraphie grecque et géographie historique du monde hellénique (sur la vie agonistique, gymnastique, epique.)" See no. 140.

1454. ***Robert, L.*** "Épitaphe d'un médicin des athlètes à Thyative. (Inscriptions de Lydie nr. 1.)" *Hellenica 9* Paris, 1950: 125-127.

1455. ***Robert, L.*** "Inscription agonistique d'Ancyre." See no. 621.

1456. ***Robert, L.*** "Inscription agonistique d'Erythrai." *RPh* 1929: 148-149 (=*OMS* 2: 1114-1115).

1457. ***Robert, L.*** "Inscription agonistique de Smyrne." See no. 622.

1458. ***Robert, L.*** "Inscriptions agonistiques Hierocésarée, nr. 6-13." See no. 620.

1459. ***Robert, L.*** "Inscriptions agonistiques d'Athènes." *RPh* 1944: 18-21 (=*OMS* 3: 1384-1387).

1460. ***Robert, L.*** "Inscriptions agonistiques de Philippopolis." *RPh* 1929: 152-155 (=*OMS* 2: 1119-1121).

1461. ***Robert, L.*** "Inscriptions agonistiques de Tralles." *RPh* 1930: 31-35 (=*OMS* 2: 1131-1135).

1462. ***Robert, L.*** "Inscriptions de la statue d'un agonothète. Thyatire, nr. 24." *Hellenica* 6 (1948): 72-75.

1463. ***Robert, L.*** "Inscriptions et institutions agonistiques I. *Aristoníkes.* II. Fêtes et magistrates de Tralles." *Eos* 48, 2 (1957): 229-238. (Symbolae Taubenschlag = *OMS* 1: 644-653).

1464. ***Robert, L.*** "Monnaies et concours de Laodicée du Lykos." See no. 623.

1465. ***Robert, L.*** *Opera minora selecta.* vols I-IV. Amsterdam: Hakkert, 1969-1974.

1466. ***Robert, L.*** "Sur les inscriptions de Chios 3. Inscription agonistique." See no. 624.

1467. ***Robert, L.*** "Sur une inscription agonistique de Thespies." See no. 625.

1468. ***Robert, L.*** "Une inscription agonistique attribué à Carycos de Cilicie." *RPh* 50 (1976): 181-192.

1469. ***Segre, M.*** "Note epigrafiche. I. Mitridate e Chio." *Mondo Classico* 2 (1932): 129-132.

1470. ***Tod, M. N.*** "Three New *SPHAIREIS* Inscriptions." See no. 987.

1470a. ***West, A. B.***, *Corinth.* See no. 542a.

1471. ***Woodward, A. M.*** "Inscriptiones Graecae V 1: Some Afterthoughts." *ABSA* 43 (1948): 209-259.

XIII

ATHLETICS IN LITERATURE

A. Homer

In addition to the following general studies on Homer and athletics, see Section II B above for works on more specific problems.

1472. ***Kornexl, E.*** "Leibesuebungen bei Homer und Platon." *Studientexte zur Leibeserziehung* 5, 1969: 48.

1473. ***Lutz, H.*** *Beitraege zur Frage der Leibesuebungen und zur Erklaerung einzelner Stellen in Homers Odyssee.* Phil. Diss.: Erlangen, 1927.

1474. ***Pope, A.*** *Die Gymnmastik bei Homer und ihre grundlagende Bedeutung fuer die Gestaltung der spaeteren Gymnastik.* See no. 221.

1475. ***Sanin, Ju. V.*** *Les Jeux Olympiques et la poésie des Hellènes.* See no. 426.

1476. ***Willimczik, K.*** *Leibesuebungen bei Homer.* See no. 229.

B. Xenophanes

1477. ***Bowra, Sir C. M.*** "Xenophanes and the Olympic Games." *AJPh* 59 (1938): 257-279. See also: id. *Problems in Greek Poetry.* (1953): 15-37.

1478. ***Marcovich, M.*** "Xenophanes on Drinking Parties and Olympic Games." See no. 263.

C. Pindar

1479. ***Bowra, Sir C. M.*** *Pindar.* Oxford: Clarendon Press, 1964. See esp. ch. 4, "The Athletic Ideal."

1480. ***Farnell, L. R.*** *The Works of Pindar.* London, 1930-1932.

1481. ***Gerber, D. E.*** *A Bibliography of Pindar: 1513-1966.* APA Monograph 28. Ann Arbor: Case Western Univ. Press, 1969. "Games": 143-144.

1482. ***Juethner, J.*** "Zu Pindar Nem. 7, 70ff." *WS* 50 (1932): 166-170.

1483. ***Kramer, K.*** *Studien zur griechischen Agonistik nach den Epiniken Pindars.* Diss.: University of Cologne, Cologne, 1970.

1484. ***Lee, H. M.*** "The TERMA and the Javelin in Pindar, Nemean vii. 70-3, and Greek Athletics." See no. 767.

1485. ***Lloyd-Jones, H.*** "Modern Interpretations of Pindar. The Second Pythian and Seventh Nemean odes." *JHS* 93 (1973): 109-137.

1486. ***Segal, C. P.*** "Pindar's Seventh Nemean." *TAPA* 98 (1967): 431-480.

1487. ***Segal, C. P.*** "Two Agonistic Problems in Pindar, Nemean, 7.70-74 and Pythian 1, 42-45. *GRBS* 9, No. 1 (1968): 31-45.

1488. ***Thummer, E.*** "Pindaros. 3. Bericht, umfassend die Jahre 1967-1972." *AAHG* 27 (1974): 1-34. Review of Pindaric scholarship. See previous reviews in *AAHG* 19 (1966): 289-322 for 1959-1966, and *AAHG* 11 (1958): 65-88 for 1945-1957.

1489. ***Woloch, M.*** "Athenian Trainers in the Aeginetan Odes of Pindar and Bacchylides." *CW* 56 (1963): 102-104 & 121.

1490. ***Wuest, E.*** *Pindar als geschichtsschreibender Dichter. Interpretation der 12 vorsizilischen Siegeslieder, des sechsten Paians und der zehnten olympischen Ode.* Diss.: Tuebingen, 1967.

D. Plato

1491. ***Bebernitz.*** "Platons Stellung zur Gymnastik." *Monatschrift fuer das Turnwesen* 7 (1888): 225-230, 297-307, 8 (1889): 186-203, 239-259, 296-305.

1492. ***Benkendorf, K. A.*** *Untersuchungen zu den platonischen Gleichnissen aus den Bereich der Gymnastik und Agonistik.* Diss.: Tuebingen, 1966.

1493. ***Kornexl, E.*** "Leibesuebungen, bei Homer und Platon." See no. 1472.

1494. ***Mehl, E.*** "Was bedeutet der Satz Platons "Einfach sei die Gymnastik."?" *Die Leibesuebungen* 5 (1929): 184.

1495. ***Meinburg, E.*** "Gymnastische Erziehung in der Platonischen Erziehung." See no. 265.

1496. ***Oppitz, R.*** *Platons Stellungnahme zu den Leibesuebungen.* Phil. Diss.: Graz, 1939.

1497. ***Ridgeway, W.*** "The Game of Polis and Plato's Republic 422 E." See no. 1023.

1498. ***Weirich, R.*** *Koerper und Koerpererziehung bei Plato.* Munich: Ph. D. diss., 1932.

E. Virgil

1499. ***Briggs, W. W. Jr.*** "Augustan Athletics and the Games of Aeneid 5." *Arena (=Stadion)* 1 (1975): 267-283.

1500. ***Lamarche, J.*** *Les sports dans l'Enéide, Chant 5.* Paris, 1937.

1501. ***Mehl, E.*** "Die Leichenspiele in der Aeneis als turngeschichtliche Quelle." *RE* 8 A, 2. Stuttgart, 1958: 1487-1493.

1502. ***Stegen, G.*** "Un match de pugilat par Virgile." See no. 865.

1503. ***Williams, R. D., ed.*** *P. Vergili Maronis Aeneidos, Liber Quintus.* Oxford, 1960.

F. Galen

1504. ***Fetz, F.*** and ***L.*** *Gymnastik bei Philostratos und Galen.* (*Studientexte zur Leibeserziehung* 4.) Frankfurt/M, 1969.

1505. ***Frank, B.*** *Die Lehren des griechischen Arzt Galen ueber Leibesuebungen.* Diss.: Dresden, 1868.

1506. ***Goehler, J.*** "Sport als Beruf - die leidenschaftliche Anklage des Kl. Galenos." *Die Leibeserziehung* 1 (1955): 164-168.

1507. ***Heubaum, R.*** "Ueber Galens 'Spiel mit dem kleinen Ball' und seine groesste Streitschrift gegen die Athleten." See no. 964.

1508. ***Korte, W.*** "Galen ueber die Leibesuebungen." Die Leibesuebungen 4 (1928): 209-210.

1509. ***Lesky, E.*** "Galen als Vorlaeufer der Hormonforschung." *Centaurus* 1 (1950): 156-162.

1510. ***Merker, J.*** "Die griechische Arzt Galen und das Ballspiel." See no. 975.

1511. ***Nickel, D.*** "Ein Ballspiel im Urteil des Arztes." See no. 977.

G. Philostratus

1512. ***Fetz, F.*** and ***L.*** *Gymnastik bei Philostratos und Galen.* See no. 1504.

1513. ***Harris, H. A.*** "Philostratus, *Imagines* I, 24, 2." *CR* 11 (1961): 3-5.

1514. ***Juethner, J.*** "Der Gymnastikos des Philostratos. Eine textgeschichtliche und textkritische Untersuchung." *SAWW* 903: 1 (vol. 145) Vienna, 1903.

1515. ***Juethner, J.*** "Gymnastisches in Philostrats *Eikones.*" *Eranos Vindbonensis* 1893: 309-330.

1516. ***Juethner, J.*** *Philostratus, Ueber Gymnastik.* Leipzig-Berlin: Teubner, 1969 reprint of 1909 ed.

1517. ***Noccelli, V.*** *Philostratus. La ginnastica.* (tr. and comm.) I class. dell'educ. fis. e dello sport I Napoli. Naples: Ed. Hermes, 1955.

1518. ***Palffy, Gy.*** "Philostratos: A tréneri tudományról Fordîtotta és jegyzetekkel elátta -." *Testneveléstudomány* 1 (1928): 38-48, 109-116, 178-186, 258-265, 371-378.

1519. ***Woody, T.*** "Philostratus: Concerning Gymnastics." *Research Quarterly* 10 (1936): 3-26.

H. Others

1520. ***Anderson, J. K.*** *Ancient Greek Horsemanship.* See no. 885.

1521. ***Anderson, J. K.*** "Notes on some Points in Xenophon's *Peri hippikes.*" *JHS* 80 (1960): 1-9.

1522. ***Berger, M.*** and ***Moussat, E.*** *Anthologie des textes sportifs de l'antiquité.* Paris, 1927.

1523. ***Boehm, J.*** *Die Leibesuebungen im Dionysepos des Nonnos von Panopolis.* Diss.: Wien, 1948.

1524. ***Buesgen, P.*** *De gymnasii Vitruvii palaestra.* Bonn, 1863.

1525. ***Cazzaniga, I.*** "Ossetvazioni critische intorno ai P. Oxy. 466e etc." See no. 814.

1526. ***Dellisanti, F.*** *L'atletismo nella critica e nella satira classica.* Fano Tip. Soniniana, 1934.
Review: AP 1936: *MC* 1936: 83 Gervasoni & 394 Oddo.

1527. ***Desmed, R.*** "Une leçon de gymnastique au IIe siècle de notre ère." *Prométhée Rev. d'Educ.* éd. par les Amis de l'École Norm. Ch. Buls (Bruxelles) 26, 1 févr. 1956: 914-915.

1528. ***Diels, H.*** "Ueber die Excerpte von Menons *Iatrika* in dem Londoner Papyrus, 137." *Hermes* 28 (1893): 407-434.

1529. ***Diem, C.*** "Epiktets Lebens- und Sportbrevier." *Olympisches Feuer* 7 (1951) 12: 28ff.

1530. ***Diem, C.*** "Heliodors Athiopika." Ein Antiker Sportroman." *Olympische Rundschau* 13 April 1941 (=*Olympische Flamme 11:* 550-564).

1531. ***Diem, C.*** "Un roman sportif de l'Antiquité. Les Ethiopique d'Héliodore." *Olympische Rundschau* 14 (1941): 8-21.

1532. ***Diem, C.*** "Philosoph Dion Chrysostomos." *Olympische Rundschau* H.22 (1943): 13-22 (=*Olympische Flamme* 2 : 586-602).

1533. ***Diem, C.*** "Le philosophe Dion Chrysostome." *Olympische Rundschau* 22 (1943): 23-29.

1534. ***Forbes, C. A.*** *"Hoi aph' Herakléous* in Epictetus and Lucianus." *AJPh* 60 (1939): 473-474.

1535. ***Gauger, F.*** *Zeitschilderung und Topik bei Juvenal.* Diss.: Greifswald, 1936.

1536. ***Gerstinger, H.*** "Das 'Faustkaempferdiplom' des Boxers Herminos alias Moros aus Hermopolis Magna." *Leibeserziehung in der Kultur.* Festschrift d. Instituts fuer Leibeserziehung, Univ. Graz. 1954: 48ff. (Summary in *AAWW* 91 (1954: 57-61.)

1537. ***Goellmann, C.*** *Zur Beurteilung der oeffentlichen Spiele. Roms bei Tacitus, Plinus dem Jungeren, Martial und Juvenal.* See no. 1122.

1538. ***Gow, A. S. F.*** *Theocritus.* Oxford, 1952.[2]

1539. ***Greco, F.*** *L'educazione fisica nella poesia, nella letterature e nell'arte greca.* See no. 1324.

1540. ***Greifenhagen, A.*** *Ein Satyrspiel des Aischylos?* 118. Winckelmannsprogramm d. Archaeol. Gesellschaft zu Berlin, 1963.

1541. ***Gruendel, L.*** "Im Quellgebiet des Sportes. Eine Umschau bei Homer." *HfL* 9 (1929): 57-61.

1542. ***Gryglewicz, F.*** "Métaphores sportives chez Saint Paul." See no. 1152.

1543. ***Hagopian, D.*** *Pollux' Faustkampf mit Amykos. Theokrits Darstellung von demselben, vergleichen mit derjenigen des Apollonius Rhodius.* See no. 842.

1544. ***Harris, H. A.*** "An Athletic *Hapax legomenon.*" *JHS* 88 (1968): 138-139.

1545. ***Harris, H. A.*** "A Fragment for the *Larisaioi* of Sophocles." *CR* 24 (1974): 4-5.

1546. ***Harris, H. A.*** "An Olympic Epigram. The Athletic Feats of Phaylos." See no. 701.

1547. ***Husner, F.*** "Leib und Seele in der Sprache Senecas." Philologus Suppl., 17, vol. 3. Leipzig, 1924.

1548. ***Jakobinyi, P.*** *A görög sport. Lukianos müve a tornászatról. Fordîtotta, bevezetéssel és jegyzetekkel ellátta (Greek Sport: Lucian's Book on Gymnastics.)* --. Budapest. No year given.

1549. ***Kannengiesser, Ch.*** "Une leçon d'athlétisme. Saint Paul commenté par les Pères." See no. 1156.

1550. ***Keresztényi, J.*** *Úymutató az ókori testkultúra tudományos kultatásához.- (A Guide to the Investigation of Ancient Physical Culture.) Guide à la recherche scientifique sur la culture physique de l'antiquité.* Budapest, 1966.

1551. ***Kopp, J. V.*** *Das physikalische Weltbild der fruehen griechischen Dichtung. Ein Beitrag zum Verstaendnis der vorsokratischen Physik.* Diss.: Freiburg i. d. Schw. Pauluschr., 1939.

Reviews: AP 1942-44: *DLZ* 1942: 107-110 Gundel. *Lychnos* 1942 386-387 Rudberg. AP 1939: *AC* 1939: 470 des places. *PhW* 1939: 1073-1077 Steiner.

1552. ***Kornexl, E.*** "Begriff und Einschaetzung der Gesundheit des Koerpers in der griechischen Literatur von ihren Anfaengen bis zum Hellenismus." See no. 258.

1553. ***Lacombrade, C.*** "En marge de Sophocle. Une course de quadriges aux jeux pythiques." *Pallas* 8 (1959): 5-14.

1554. ***Laemmer, M.*** *"Parodeuo bei gymnaschen Agonen." ZPE* 1 (1967): 105-106.

1555. ***Leitner, H.*** *A Bibliography to the Ancient Medical Authors.* Bern and Stuttgart: Huber, 1973.

1556. ***Lochner-Huettenbach, F.*** "Bilder und Vergleiche aus dem Sportwesen in der spaeten griechischen Epik." *Hans Gerstinger - Festgabe zum 80. Geburstag. Arbeiten aus dem Grazer Schuelerkreis.* Graz Acad, Dr. - & Verl.-Anst., 1967: 31-40.

1557. ***Lochner-Huettenbach, F.*** "Sportgleichnisse in der archaischen Epik und Lyrik der Griechen." *Festschrift J. Recla.* Graz Inst. fuer Leibeserziehung der Univ., 1965: 44-57.

1558. ***Mann, J. C.*** *"Gymnazo* in Thucydides 1. 6. 5-6." *CR* 24 (1974): 177-178.

1559. ***Mering, W.*** *Die Anschauungen des Hippokrates ueber Gymnastik und Massage.* Diss.: Munich, 1937.

1560. ***Mezey, S.*** *Pausanias Olympiája az ásatások világában.* Temesvár, 1907.

1561. ***Miller, S. G.*** *Arete.* See no. 111.

1562. ***Musiolek, P.*** "Die Anschauungen des Aristotle ueber koerperliche Erziehung als Teil der Paideia in ihrem historischen Zusammenhang." See no. 268.

1563. ***Muth, R.*** "Die Olympischen Spiele in der Dichtung der Hellenen." *Olympia einst und jetzt. Vortragsreihe der Universitaet Innsbruck und des Kulturamtes der Stadt Innsbruck aus Anlass der 9 Olympischen Winterspiele 1964.* Schriftleit. Muth, R., Zusammenstell. des Bildteiles, Wotschitzky, A. Innsbruck Selbstverl. des Stadtmagistrates, 1964: 37-53.

1564. ***Ortega, A.*** "Metáforas del deporte griego en S. Pablo." See no. 1166.

1565. ***Peek, W.*** "Delphische Gedichte." See no. 514.

1566. ***Peek, W.*** "Zu griechischen Epigrammen." *Hermes* 74 (1944): 220-222.

1567. ***Pfitzner, V. C.*** "Paul and the Agon Motif. Traditional Athletic Imagery in Pauline Literature." See no. 1170.

1568. ***Piernavieja del Pozo, M.*** "El deporte en la literatura latina. Antologia." *CAF Rev. del Com. Olimpico Esp. Madrid* 2 (1960): 417-596.

1569. ***Piernavieja, R. P.*** "*Ludia,* un terme sportif latin chez Juvénal et Martial." *Latomus* 31 (1972): 1037-1040.

1570. ***Radt, S. L.*** "Iets over de betekenis van de Grote Spelen voor de Griekse litteratuur." *Hermeneus* 31 (1960): 214-219.

1571. ***Ritook, Zs.*** *Színház és stadion. (Theater and Stadium.) Osszeállította, az elöszót és a jegyzeteket írta* Budapest, 1968.
(Európai Antológia-Görögország).

1572. ***Robert, L.*** "Les épigrammes satiriques de Lucilius sur les athlétés: parodie et réalités." *Entretiens sur l'Antiquité Classique. Tome 14. L'épigramme grecque.* Gent (Fondation Hardt), 1968: 181-291.

1573. ***Robinson, R. S.*** *Sources for the History of Greek Athletics in English Translation.* See no. 141.

1574. ***Sanin, Ju. V.*** *Les Jeux Olympiques et la poésie des Hellènes.* See no. 426.

1575. ***Soveri, H. F.*** *De ludorum memoria praecipue Tertullianea. Capita selecta.* Helsingforsia: ex officina Societatis litterariae fennicae, 1912: 157-160.

1576. ***Steindl, E.*** (intro. and tr.) *Lukian. Leibesuebungen in alten Athen (Anacharsis).* Zurich: Artemis, 1962.

1577. ***Sutton, D. F.*** "Athletics in the Greek Satyr Play." *RSC* 23 (1975): 203-209.

1578. ***Thomas, E.*** "Ovid at the Races. *Amores* III, 2; *Ars Amatoria* I, 135-164." *Hommages à M. Renard.* I, pp. 710-724, ed. J. Bibauw, Coll. Latomus. Brusseles: 1969.

1579. ***Welskopf, E. Ch.*** "Die Krise des Sports im Spiegel der Literatur und der Philosophie." *Hellenische Poleis.* Welskopf, E. Ch., ed. Berlin: Akad.-Verl., 1974: 1484-1489.

1580. ***Widdra, K. O.*** *Xenophons "Reitkunst".* See no. 930.

1581. ***Wilcken, U.*** "Ein Faustkaempfer-Diplom." *Grundzuege und Chrestomathie des Papyruskunde.* Mitteis, L. and Wilcken, U., eds. Leipzig and Berlin, 1912. 1, 2: 184-187, nr. 156.

1582. ***Wilcken, U.*** "Liquidationsgesuch eines agonistischen Siegers an den Rat." *Grundzuege und Chrestomathie des Papyruskunde.* Mitteis, L. and Wilcken, U. eds. Leipzig and Berlin, 1912. 1, 2.: 187-188, nr. 157.

1583. ***Wilcken, U.*** "Verleihung von Immunitaeten an den Sproessling einer Athletenfamilie." *Grundzuege und Chrestomathie des Papyruskunde.* Mitteis, L. and Wilcken, U., eds. Leipzig and Berlin, 1912. 1, 2: 199-198, nr. 158.

1584. ***Wilhelm, H. E.*** "Lukian als Zeuge fuer hellenische Sportauffassung." *LKE* 54 (1935): 483-484.

1585. ***Willis, W. H.*** "Athletic Contests in the Epic." *TAPA* 72 (1941): 392-417.

1586. ***Woloch, M.*** "Athenian Trainers in the Aeginetan Odes of Pindar and Bacchylides." See no. 1489.

XIV

ATHLETICS: OTHER ANCIENT AND MODERN SOCIETIES

1587. ***Baran M.*** "Children's Games." *Expedition* 17 (1974): 21-23.

1588. ***Bastholm, E.*** *The History of Muscle Physiology.* Acta Historica Scient. Natur. & Medecin. 7. Copenhagen: Munksgaard, 1950.

1589. ***Boutros, L.*** *Phoenician Sport. Its Influence on the Origin of the Olympic Games.* See no. 451.

1590. ***Curtius, L.*** "Moderner und antiker sport." *Deutsches Volkstum* 1928: 584-591.

1591. **Diem, C.** "Antiker und Moderner Sport." *AA* 1959: 357-364.

1592. ***Diem, C.*** *Gymnastischer Dreiklang. Antike, Asien, Jetztzeit. Koerperkultur dieser Zeiten und Voelker nach ihrem Leitungsbilde beurteilt.* Schriftenreihe des internat. Olymp. Inst. Berlin 2. Berlin: Limpert, 1938.

1593. ***Gedda, L.*** *Lo Sport.* See no. 43.

1594. ***Huizinga, J.*** *Homo Ludens.* See no. 59.

1595. ***Jakob-Rost, L.*** "Sport im Alten-Orient?" *Altertum* 11 (1965): 3-8.

1596. ***Jankovich, M.*** *They Rode into Europe. The Fruitful Exchange in the Arts of Horsemanship between East and West.* See no. 899.

1597. ***Jegel, A.*** "Alte und neue Gymnastik als Helferin der Eugenik." *Dt. mediz Wochenschr.* 61 (1935): 2022-2025.

1598. ***Juethner, J.*** "Die koerperliche Erziehung im Altertum und Neuzeit." *LKE* 15 (1939): 448-453.

1599. ***Jung, A.*** *Massage und Sport im Altertum und Gegenwart.* See no. 74.

1600. ***Lucas, G.*** "Athletentypen." See no. 93.

1601. ***Lukas, G.*** *Die Koerperkultur in fruehen Epochen der Menscheitsentwicklung.* See no. 94.

1602. ***Luther, W.*** "Die griechische Gymnastik als Leitbild fuer Sport und Spiel im Gymnasium der Gegenwart." See no. 95.

1603. ***Méautis, G.*** "Sports antiques et sports modernes." See no. 101.

1604. ***Morgan, M. G.*** "Three Non-Roman Blood Sports." *CQ* 25 (1975): 117-122.

1605. ***Niedermann, E.*** "Moeglichkeiten und Grenzen einer Chronologie der Weltgeschichte des Sports." *Stadion* 3 (1977): 312-315.

1606. ***Patrucco, R.*** *La psicologia dell'atleta.* See no. 117.

1607. ***Renson, R., Nayer, P. P. de,*** and ***Ostin, M., eds.*** *The History, Evolution and Diffusion of Sports and Games in Different Cultures.* See no. 137.

1608. ***Riemschneider, M.*** "Spielbrett und Spielbeutel in Antike und Mittelalter." *Acta ethnogr. Acad. Scient.Hung.* 8, 3-4 (1959): 309-326. See German summary in *BCO* 5 (1960): 339-341.

1609. ***Saubier, B.*** and ***Stahr, E.*** *Geschichte der Leibesuebungen.* See no. 149.

1610. ***Schiessling, S.*** *Wertschaetzung der Gymnastik bei den Griechen und Wuerdigung der koerperlichen Ausbildung der Jugend der Neuenzeit.* Mies, 1891-92.

1611. ***Schroeder, B.*** "Antike Gymnastik und moderner Sport." *Schoenheit* 25 (1930): 486-490.

1612. ***Servadio, E.*** "Sport." See no. 153.

1613. ***Ulmann, J.*** "De la gymnastique aux sports modernes. Histoire des doctrines de l'éducation physique." *BHM* 42 (1968): 283-284.

1614. ***Velgus, V. A.*** "Jugglers of Ancient Egypt and Alexandrian Jugglers in China." (in Russian with an English summary) *Basic Problems of African Studies, in Honor of D. A. Olderogge* (in Russian with English summary) Inst. of Ethnogr. of the U.S.S.R. Acad. of Sc. Moscow: Ed. Nanka, 1973: 312-323.

1615. ***Weiler, I.*** *Der Sport bei den Voelker der alten Welt. Eine Einfuehrung.* See no. 170.

ADDENDA

163[a]. *Ulf, C.* "Die Einreibung der griechischen Athleten mit Oel. Zweck und Ursprung." *Stadion* 5 (1979): 220-238.

184[a]. ***Coulomb, J.*** "Les Boxeurs minoens." *BCH* 105 (1981): 27-40.

389[a]. ***Matthews, V. J.*** "Sulla and the Games of the 175th Olympiad (80 B.C.)." *Stadion* 5 (1979): 239-243.

455[a]. ***Lacroix, L.*** "La Légende de Pelops et son iconographie." *BCH* 100 (1976): 327-341.

555[a]. ***Miller, S. G.*** 1"Kleonai, the Nemean Games, and the Lamian War." Pages 100ff. in *Hesperia Suppl. XX* (1982).

584[a]. ***Davaras, K.*** "Das Grab eines kretischen Wettkampfsiegers? Vorlaüfiger Ausgrabungsbericht." *Stadion* 5 (1979): 193-219.

631[a]. ***Weiss, P.*** "Ein agonistisches Bema und die isopythischen Spiele von Side." *Chiron* 11 (1981): 315-346.

631[b]. ***Williams, C. K.***, and ***Russell, P.*** "Corinth Excavations of 1980." Includes the sports complex. *Hesperia* 50 (1981): 1-44.

646[a]. ***Frost, F. J.*** "The Dubious Origins of the 'Marathon'." *AJAH* 4 (1979): 179-163.

649[a]. ***Hausmann, U., ed.*** *Der Tuebinger Waffenlauefer.* Tuebingen, 1977= Tuebinger Studien zur Archaeologie und Kunstgeschichte, Bd. 4.

1109[a]. ***Wisseman, S. U.*** *The Archaeological Evidence for Etruscan Games.* Ph.D. Dissertation. Bryn Mawr College, 1981.

1206[a]. ***Goceva, Z.*** "Epigraphische Zeugnisse zu den Gladiatorenkaempfen in der Provinz Thrakien." *Altertum* 27 (1981): 88-93.

1333[a]. ***Hoenle, A.*** and ***Henze, A.*** *Roemische Amphitheatre und Stadien. Gladiatorenkaempfe und Circusspiele.* Edition *Antike Welt.* Zurich, 1981.

1389[a]. ***Thomas, Renate.*** *Athletenstatuetten der Spaetarchaik und des strengen Stils.* Vorwart von H. G. Neimeyer. Archaeologica 18. Rome, 1981.

1484[a]. ***Lee, H. M.*** "Athletic Arete in Pindar." *AncW* 7 (1983): 31-37.

1523[a]. ***Brown, T. S.*** "Herodotus' Views on Athletics." *AncW* 7 (1983): 17-29.

1574[a]. ***Scanlon, T. F.*** "Olympic Dust, the Delphic Laurel, and Isthmian Toil: Horace and Greek Athletics." *Arete* 1.2 (1984): in press.

INDEX OF AUTHORS

(Reference is to Nos of entries. Some Nos added too late for inclusion in the text and marked with a([a]) or a ([b]), e.g. 163[a], refer to the addenda page 129)

COMPLETE YOUR LIBRARY

$10.00

DAVID YOUNG

THE OLYMPIC MYTH OF GREEK AMATEUR ATHLETICS

ISBN: 0-89005-523-8

No amateur ever competed at the ancient Olympics. All Greek athletes competed for prizes, with no restriction on winnings. Many ancient athletic meets paid cash or in-kind prizes. At the games in Plato's Athens, the men's 200-meter victor won a prize worth $67,000.

The Olympics awarded a mere olive crown. But in 600 B.C., Athens paid any Athenian winning at Olympia a cash prize of $300,000. Other cities did the same. If we prefer "amateurism" for our own Olympics, that is our choice. But we must stop blaming the ancient Greeks. They didn't even have a word for it.

This book has arisen from a need to put into the hands of the students ancient readings which provide evidence for and reveal various aspects of Greek athletes. These students who are, for the most part, with no prior experience of classics and the Classical world are eager and willing to confront the problems of a lack or conflicting evidence from antiquity, but they do not have the ancient languages necessary to do so. This book should be used together with a handbook such as Gardiner's *Athletics of the Ancient World* which will provide a general background of the physical evidence for the study of the Greek Athletics.

Just Mail your order form to: **ARES PUBLISHERS, INC.,**

ORDER FORM

NAME ____________________

ADDRESS ____________________

CITY ____________________ STATE __________ ZIP ____________________

COUNTRY ____________________

QUANTITY	AUTHOR	TITLE	PRICE	
		Postage/Handling	1	.50
		Total		

Send your order to:

ARES PUBLISHERS INC.
7020 NORTH WESTERN AVE.
CHICAGO, ILLINOIS 60645